DELHI DARSHAN

DELHI DARSHAN

The History and Monuments of India's Capital

Giles Tillotson

PENGUIN
VIKING

An imprint of Penguin Random House

VIKING

USA | Canada | UK | Ireland | Australia
New Zealand | India | South Africa | China

Viking is part of the Penguin Random House group of companies whose addresses can be found at global.penguinrandomhouse.com

Published by Penguin Random House India Pvt. Ltd
7th Floor, Infinity Tower C, DLF Cyber City,
Gurgaon 122 002, Haryana, India

First published in Viking by Penguin Random House India 2019

Copyright © Giles Tillotson 2019

All rights reserved

10 9 8 7 6 5 4 3 2 1

The views and opinions expressed in this book are the author's own and the facts are as reported by him which have been verified to the extent possible, and the publishers are not in any way liable for the same.

ISBN 9780670091911

Typeset in Adobe Garamond Pro by Manipal Digital Systems, Manipal
Printed at Thomson Press India Ltd, New Delhi

This book is sold subject to the condition that it shall not, by way of trade or otherwise, be lent, resold, hired out, or otherwise circulated without the publisher's prior consent in any form of binding or cover other than that in which it is published and without a similar condition including this condition being imposed on the subsequent purchaser.

www.penguin.co.in

To Rebekah and Hadassah

Contents

Introduction   ix

MONUMENTS IN HISTORY

The Site   3
New Foundations: The 'Slave' Dynasty   5
Expansion and Division: Khaljis and Tughluqs   24
Death in the Park: Sayyids and Lodis   38
On the River: The Great Mughals   51
Staying On: The Late Mughals   82
Starting Anew: The British   98
Partition and Growth: Independent India   117

SUGGESTED ROUTES

Shahjahanabad: Red Fort and Jami Masjid   141
Humayun's Tomb and Lodi Road   143
The Qutb Minar and Mehrauli   146
Rajpath and Janpath   150

Kashmiri Gate and Beyond	154
Central New Delhi—North	156
Central New Delhi—South	157
Rajghat to the Lotus Temple	159
Hauz Khas to Tughluqabad	161
Further Reading	165
Acknowledgements	169
Index	171

Introduction

Its origin and antiquity may be disputed, but Delhi has without doubt been a major city—even a capital city, on and off—for at least a thousand years. It has served as a centre of power for Rajput clans, for the first sultans, for Mughal emperors, for the administrators of the British Raj in the early twentieth century, and for India's federal government since Independence in 1947. Successive regimes established themselves on adjacent or overlapping sites, adding to Delhi's vertical layers and its horizontal spread. Old guidebooks speak of the 'seven cities of Delhi'; but these were all Islamic citadels, built before the coming of the British, and in recent times archaeologists have added more cities to the bottom of the tally just as developers have added many more to its top.

The Mughals built their walled city in the seventeenth century by the riverbank, as far away as topography would permit from the earliest settlements. Three centuries later the British added their geometrically planned extravagance in the mostly empty centre, between the Mughal city in the north and the ruined sultanate forts in the south. In the late twentieth century, new housing colonies filled up all the spaces in between, and in the new millennium the spread has extended beyond those historic boundary markers, both south-westwards into the farmlands of the hinterland and eastwards across the Yamuna river, to create the new satellite cities of Gurgaon and Noida. The aggregate—officially called the National Capital Region—is today among the largest and fastest-growing urban conurbations in the world.

Neither history nor geography, however, fully conveys the city's characteristic layering: the constant interaction between its present and its past. The past informs the present in obvious ways, as we live amid historic sites; but the present also informs the past in the sense that we encounter old sites in our own time, through the lens of recent use. This book, intended as an introduction for anyone who lives in or visits the city, explores its sites not only in relation to their own time, but in terms of what subsequent periods have made of them, examining some of their accumulated meanings and myths.

To residents of Delhi, for example, the famous India Gate is not just a war memorial; for a long time it has also been a favoured place to go for an ice cream on a hot summer night, and lately it has become a place where members of civil society collect to protest miscarriages of justice. Political protesters traditionally prefer to congregate at Jantar Mantar, an eighteenth-century observatory, despite periodic attempts by the authorities to prohibit its use for politics. The Lodi Gardens is not just the location of some early tombs but a place for picnicking, jogging and falling in love; it is one of the few spaces where public displays of affection are tolerated, perhaps because the relative affluence of the average Lodi Gardens visitor deters officious intervention. The Red Fort, built by the Mughal emperor Shah Jahan, now serves as the podium for an annual speech to the nation by the prime minister on Independence Day. Such later uses are as important as the original functions in explaining how the buildings are seen today.

The Purana Qila, or 'old fort', marks a point of origin or new beginning in various time zones. Built in the sixteenth century, it is by no means the oldest fort in Delhi, despite its name: it is called 'purana' because it predates the walled city of Shah Jahan and was the Mughals' first establishment in Delhi. It is also popularly believed to mark the site of Indraprastha—the capital of the Pandavas, the heroes of the Mahabharata—taking the history of the city into India's epic past. Modern excavations have indeed revealed very early pottery remains, confirming that identification for those who are willing to believe in it. But the archaeologists could move into the site only after the departure of the refugees: at the time of Independence and Partition in 1947, and for some years afterwards, the enclosed sanctuary of the Purana Qila was used as a transit camp by many who were escaping communal violence in the old city or preparing to migrate to Pakistan; and later some of those who had fled from it. Those who came from the western part of Punjab form a significant core of Delhi's senior generation, and for some of them the 'old fort' was the site of their new beginning, in a new nation.

Such layering is everywhere. Humayun's tomb is not only the burial place of one of the early Mughal emperors, it is also the place where his last ruling descendant, Bahadur Shah Zafar, was arrested, at the bloody denouement of the 1857 uprisings. Driving around the elegant avenues of New Delhi, lined by government servants' bungalows protected by high fences and armed guards, you might at first take the scene as typical of Indian officialdom: such apparent self-importance! But look again and you realize that nothing has changed since the 1930s; that this is a colonial city after all, modelled in part on a military cantonment.

On the other hand, few people today would regard Rashtrapati Bhavan (the former Viceroy's House) or the Secretariats as legacies of colonial rule: they may be massive and imperial, but they are more popularly associated with independent India's successive presidents and ministers. They are proud symbols not of the past but of the present.

Just as the past erupts into the present, so the present refashions the past according to its own compulsions. This is what makes Delhi so intriguing and makes spending time in it worthwhile. Highly congested and with poor infrastructure, Delhi is a difficult city to live or move around in, but its shortcomings fade if we have an eye for its many layers. The chapters of this book together present a concise history of the city, focusing on its most prominent people and places. A brief concluding section describes some suggested routes for exploring the city. I have avoided cluttering the text with the scholarly apparatus of notes and references. Readers who are curious about my sources for particular pieces of information and quotations, or just want to know more, can look up the section titled Further Reading.

Having thus conveyed an impression of a wish to be at once brief, authoritative and helpful, I should add that this short book is very much a personal view of Delhi which reflects my own prejudices and preoccupations. Much has been written about the city, especially in recent years, by a number of writers with a range of approaches and specialist expertise. I point to some of this in Further Reading. I have learnt from and draw from this writing; but I have made no attempt to be comprehensive or encyclopaedic. I am an architectural historian, with a range of interests in Rajput, sultanate, Mughal, colonial and modern architecture. I look at design, but I also look at how any building is rooted in history, often in more than one period. So if you share my interests in history, architecture and design—and whether you know Delhi less well, as well, or better than I do—I hope that you will find something of pleasure and profit in reading my take on it.

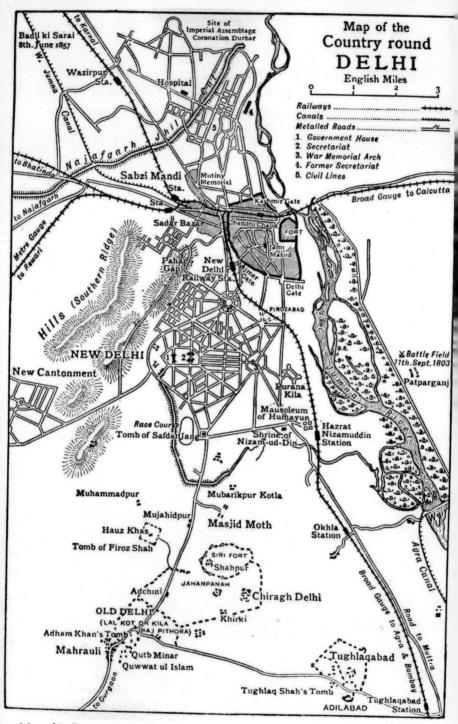

Map of Delhi c. 1930, showing the roads of New Delhi laid out between Shahjahanabad in the north and the ruined sultanate cities in the south

Monuments in History

The Site

A river flows from north to south. A range of low hills rises close to the bank at a northern point but then pursues its own diverging line to the south-west. A broken arc of high ground reconnects the hills with the river in the south, completing the boundary of a rough triangular space of flat earth. It is a natural sanctuary, at once watered and sheltered, fertile and of large extent. But no indigenous tribe inhabits this domain. Almost everyone who has ever lived here is of immigrant stock of one kind or another: the Rajput clans and Turkic invaders who built the first cities; the British who began another; the refugees from partitioned Punjab who came here in 1947; the labourers from Rajasthan and Bihar; and the middle-class hopefuls who still come from all parts of India in ever-increasing numbers. But this is no melting pot, as many communities retain their distinct identities—like the proud Punjabis—and even specific residential zones, like the cohesive Bengalis. This is Delhi, a conglomerate of cities built by rulers with dreams of unity and permanence, inhabited by a mixed and ever-changing population.

The citizens of Delhi are not bound together by ties of common culture or even language. Their sense of identity is drawn from the place itself, from the urban spaces that they share. Delhi's distinctive character is physical in kind: it consists of buildings in a landscape. The points of reference on our mental map are the forts and tombs of the Mughals; the bungalows, markets and roundabouts of the British period; and the 'bhavans', the administrative and cultural institutions of the post-Independence era. Many of the place names—even those of housing colonies like Lodi Estate—evoke ancient dynasties, the landlords of the past, as if we all live in rented houses rather than ones that we built ourselves.

The first name that we must consider in detail, though, is that of Delhi itself. Its origin and meaning are forgotten. Some historians interpret it to mean 'threshold', marking it as the point of entry into India for conquerors from the other side of the Hindu Kush. A rival claim associates it with an earlier and more local hero, Raja Dhilu. Each theory has its confident adherents but neither of them persuades everyone. What we can be sure of, though, is that the current and universally accepted spelling gained currency only in the nineteenth century and was formulated by the British. And it is wrong. It captures neither the spelling nor the pronunciation of the name in Hindi, which is more accurately rendered as 'Dilli'. The now official 'Delhi' is in fact simply a sloppy mis-transliteration of the Urdu version. A correct transliteration would be 'Dehli', which was indeed the form that was used by Europeans earlier, but was somehow lost. It is ironic that nationalist politicians, eager to cleanse the country of traces of colonialism, have changed the hybrid but euphonious names of many other cities, such as Bombay, Calcutta and Bangalore, replacing them with pedantic transliterations from the regional languages, but they have been content to leave the name of the national capital in its mangled form. Some old-fashioned scholars still call it Dehli. Subeditors correct them.

New Foundations: The 'Slave' Dynasty

In 1192, Muhammad bin Sam, the sultan of Ghur in present-day Afghanistan, crossed the Indus river. This was not his first visit to India, and an alliance of Rajput rulers in northern India—determined to make it his last—assembled its armies at Tarain to confront him. But they were defeated, and in the following year the Ghurid forces reached the Yamuna river and swept into Rajasthan to take possession of both Delhi and Ajmer, cities associated with the legendary Rajput leader Prithviraj Chauhan.

This outcome seems to have taken everyone by surprise. It inspired—either at the time or (more probably) later—an epic Rajasthani poem, the main source of our knowledge of Prithviraj, celebrating his heroism and lamenting his defeat. The conquest may even have surprised the victor himself and was probably not what he intended. His expedition was planned as a temporary raid, following a well-established pattern. A few generations earlier, in the opening decades of the twelfth century, another sultan, Mahmud of Ghazni, had made a series of almost annual incursions into India. He targeted rich temple towns because his object was not conquest but loot.

Muhammad of Ghur had already imitated this example once and possibly had the same purpose again. He certainly had no plans to settle, given India's uncongenial climate and the need to return and protect his homeland. But having occupied the Rajput territories, he left behind his principal general, Qutb-ud-din Aibak, to rule in his name as a Ghurid viceroy. Things continued in this way for over a decade with Qutb-ud-din based in Delhi. But when Muhammad of Ghur was assassinated in 1206, rather than pledging his allegiance to his successor, Qutb-ud-din declared himself independent, thus establishing a new political entity, known as the Delhi Sultanate.

The history of Delhi from this moment on is fairly well-documented. Parts of the cities built by Qutb-ud-din and his successors still survive, as do court histories that record their trials and triumphs. But it is perhaps not surprising to find that many people are dissatisfied that the history of India's capital city should begin with a defeat at foreign hands. Nationalist historians, and even dispassionate antiquarians, would like to be able to flesh out the period before the conquest. The problem is that what we have is scanty and inconclusive.

There is, to begin with, a strong and long-standing tradition that associates Delhi with Indraprastha, the capital of the Pandavas, heroes of the national epic, the Mahabharata. Believers point to a village, surviving until a hundred years ago, called Indarpat, contained within but predating the Purana Qila, a fort of the Mughal period. The site is certainly ancient, but professional historians and archaeologists tread warily in a field that mixes emotion, religion and politics. They have excavated some potsherds of a type known as 'painted greyware', which is dated to c.1000 BC, but it requires a leap of faith to see this as evidence in support of the myth.

From the more immediate pre-conquest era, we have a few names—such as that of the ruler Anang Pal—and some locations that are clearly connected with them, such as Anangpur. We have coins and potsherds. There are even some significant monuments, like the large masonry reservoir known as the Suraj Kund, believed to have been built in the tenth century. But these fragments of history are strung together by doubts and questions, rather than by facts. Did rulers like Suraj Pal, known only from bardic sources, really exist, and if so, when? How do the kings mentioned in various inscriptions relate to each other dynastically?

Despite the uncertainty, a traditional scholarly view persists that Delhi's oldest and probably first fortification wall, known as Lal Kot, located at the south-western extremity of modern Delhi, was built by the Tomar Rajputs in the eleventh century. Some time in the twelfth century this fort was captured by another Rajput clan, the Chauhans, who came from Sambhar in Rajasthan. The most famous member of this dynasty, Prithviraj, also known as Rai Pithora, doubled the size of Lal Kot and renamed it after himself, Qila Rai Pithora, only to lose it soon afterwards to the invading armies of Muhammad of Ghur.

This inconvenient historical episode cannot be undone but it can be symbolically reversed. In 2002 (that is 810 years after the event), a section of crumbling wall, identified as part of Qila Rai Pithora, was patched up, and the Delhi Development Authority replaced the surrounding debris with verdant landscaping to create a public park. At its heart, perched on top of a rather uninspiring interpretation centre, is an enormous bronze equestrian statue of Prithviraj, bow and arrow at the ready, all set to reconquer. Even the pigeons—its most numerous devotees—look restless. The whole complex was inaugurated by L.K. Advani, at the time minister of home affairs in the central government, and a prominent member of the Bharatiya Janata Party, which was then (as now) widely perceived as adept at harnessing Hindu religious sentiment. A nearby information board mentions the Chauhan capture of Delhi from the Tomars and describes the extended Qila Rai Pithora as 'the first of the so-called seven cities of Delhi'. Er . . . one second. That phrase about the seven cities was coined by colonial-era historians to describe the sultanate and Mughal sites. There is today a well-established practice of pseudo-scholarship that involves reattributing Islamic monuments to Hindu authorship. But there is a nuance here. There really was a pre-existing fort that the Ghurid forces captured and used, so in this case the reattribution is not unreasonable. Even so, deciding that a given stretch of wall was a part of Prithviraj's fort and sticking a massive statue of him on it rather smacks of trying to replace the monuments of Delhi's missing Hindu past.

The Ghurid general, Qutb-ud-din Aibak, developed the fort that he had wrested from Prithviraj Chauhan, strengthening its defences and constructing within it the new buildings required for the first capital of the sultanate. These included a congregational mosque, aptly (though probably only later) named Quwwatu'l-Islam, the 'Might of Islam', and the towering Qutb Minar, standing at its south-eastern corner.

Some of the material remains of the Rajput period survive in recycled form. As the archaeologist Y.D. Sharma noted, an inscription at the eastern entrance proudly records how no fewer than twenty-seven Hindu and Jain temples, perhaps dating from the Tomar period, which once stood in the Qila Rai Pithora or in its vicinity, were demolished to provide material for the building of the Quwwatu'l-Islam. The colonnade that encloses the mosque's earliest and inner courtyard is entirely composed of temple columns. Though here redeployed in the service of a different religion, they still bear the carvings that relate to their former use: depictions of hanging bells, overflowing pots, the mask-like *kirtimukha* or 'face of fortune', abundant foliage and even, in a few cases, figures of human form. It is hard to know whether Qutb-ud-din appreciated this exquisite work. Many of the columns have been cut and reassembled to make them fit, which hardly suggests a connoisseur's eye, and it is possible that the carving was once concealed under plaster. Some Hindu idols were originally inserted face down at the thresholds, which indicates a more plausible interpretation of the whole project as a gesture of intimidation over those he had conquered. So too does the Qutb Minar, the tower that stands outside but looms over the courtyard. Nearly 240 feet high, this minar is rather taller than is required for the muezzin to give the call to prayer—indeed anyone calling from the top would go unheard—and it makes more sense as a splendid tower of victory. It certainly casts a long shadow.

There is much nervousness in academic circles these days about building episodes of this kind. There are many instances across north India of temple parts having being reused in mosque construction. Historians used to just refer to the stones as 'spolia' and move on. But the violent demolition in 1992 by Hindu fanatics of a mosque in Ayodhya that had been built by the Mughal emperor Babur, supposedly on the site of a demolished temple, stirred tensions in Indian society that have still not subsided. The history of Hindu-Muslim relations has itself become a battlefield, contested in the present by various political and religious parties as well as by rival schools of historians. One of the leaders of the Ayodhya temple movement was the same L.K. Advani who ten years later so valiantly recalled Prithviraj to Delhi. Nowadays, while many people believe that Muslim invaders destroyed temples in large quantities, serious historians mostly prefer to play the matter down, suggesting that religious differences in India became marked only during the period of British rule. Any account of history that points to communal divisions is liable to meet with censure in certain academic circles. One historian went so far as to list all the verifiable cases of temple destruction, in an effort to demonstrate that they were few, while running the risk of adding

Reused temple columns in the aisles of the Quwwatu'l-Islam, postcard by H.A. Mirza & Sons c. 1910

fuel to the fire by pointing out exactly where they were. In my view, it might be more sensible to admit that religious differences sometimes did spark violence in the past, while deploring those who invoke such moments as a model or justification for their own actions now. Some devout Hindus ask, 'Since the Muslims destroyed so many temples, may we not rebuild just one?' But no one would stop at one. Those who seek to redress the past allow themselves to be enslaved by it.

An earlier response to the religiously inspired architectural aggression of Qutb-ud-din—a response that is no more satisfactory than pretending it doesn't exist—was to turn the whole matter round and claim that the Qutb Minar was built not by Qutb-ud-din at all but by the defeated Prithviraj Chauhan. This line of thought gained adherents with the rise of Indian nationalism in the late nineteenth century. Various specious arguments were advanced to show how its features conformed to early Rajput architecture, an exercise that involved overlooking its much closer resemblance to prototypes in Afghanistan. An unlikely early proponent of the theory—writing in his youth in the 1840s and trying to be non-partisan—was Syed Ahmad Khan, later to emerge as an influential Muslim reformer and educator.

In one sense—though not in the sense they mean—those who challenge the identity of particular buildings have a point in this case. If Qutb-ud-din, by building his mosque out of dismantled temples, intended a gesture of mastery and control, then it rebounded on him as the temple columns give the mosque a decidedly Indian character. The colonnades do not look like parts of a mosque in any other country where Islam had spread. Some such thought seems to have struck Qutb-ud-din (or some think his successor) because a screen of high-pointed arches, modelled on the buildings of Seljuq Persia, was added as an afterthought across the front of the prayer hall, screening some of the columns from view. The idea seems to have been that inserting a row of pointed arches across the western side, towards which the devout faced while at prayer, would make the whole thing look less like a temple and more like a mosque.

Up to a point, it does, but even this revision was not entirely satisfactory. The arches may have the pointed outline that is distinctive of Islamic architecture worldwide, but the technology of arch construction was little known, if at all, in India at this time, and the Indian masons employed to do the job used their own traditional trabeate (post and beam) system. The arches are composed not of voussoirs (wedge-shaped pieces arranged like a fan) but of horizontal layers of stone, carved into shape. Variations in the colour of the stone make this visible even on a casual inspection from the ground. As a result, the screen may be more Islamic in appearance than the rest of the mosque, but it is still Indian in method.

Approaching the screen reveals Indian hands in another respect: it is covered in carved ornamentation. Much of it—notably the swirling organic scrolls—is derived from designs customarily used in temples; not in this case plundered from actual earlier temples but made new and adapted to a new purpose. Around the arches run Quranic inscriptions. The masons have faithfully copied a calligraphic model, but they have not been able to resist adding their own flourishes, filling every available gap with scrolling creeper and bursting bud. The Arabic letters sprout Indian flora.

This early beginning set the tenor for all subsequent sultanate and Mughal architecture. The patrons might have looked beyond India's borders for inspiration or for building specialists, but they also engaged, willingly or by necessity, with Indian conditions: its climate, its building materials and the expertise of its craftsmen. This gives the Islamic buildings of India a distinctive aesthetic, despite their many similarities with the buildings of Persia and elsewhere. The architecture of the deserts of central and west Asia—composed of brick and tile—is translated on India's fertile plains into an architecture of richly carved stone, worked by Indian expert hands.

The core of the Qutb complex—the courtyard and the tower begun by the conquering general, Qutb-ud-din—is surrounded by the extensions added by his successors. Even the Qutb Minar was a joint venture. Qutb-ud-din completed only the lowest storey and the remainder—up to an original total of four—was contributed by his successor, Iltutmish, in the early thirteenth century. Through the course of the fourteenth century, the tower was struck by lightning more than once. After one such episode, in 1368, Sultan Firuz Shah Tughluq dismantled the damaged top storey and replaced it with two more, raising the total to five. He introduced white marble for the first time, perhaps to make it harmonize with the Alai Darwaza, the grand gateway that stands nearby, which had been built in 1310 by Alauddin Khalji.

Even then it was not complete. An aquatint by the English topographical artists Thomas and William Daniell, based on drawings they made on site in 1789, shows a cupola on the top. The minar was again struck by lightning in 1803, the year the British took possession of Delhi, and the cupola was destroyed.

Some years later, in the 1820s, a military engineer named Robert Smith was put in charge of Delhi's historic monuments, and he began to think about restoring them. Smith was an able draughtsman who had long been sketching Indian buildings. During a spell of leave in Britain, he met William Daniell and was evidently impressed: his own later artistic work shows the influence of the Daniells, as it is more ambitious in scale and focuses on grand architectural scenes. He took advantage of his posting in Delhi to paint large canvases of the city's major sites including the Purana Qila and the Quwwatu'l-Islam. He lived in an apartment within the old city walls with his Indian bibi, and counted among his friends James Skinner, the founder of Skinner's Horse, for whom he prepared the original designs for St. James's Church at Kashmiri Gate. From time to time, Smith was called on to exercise his military skills: during the siege of Bharatpur in 1826, he laid the mine that blew the fort. But back in Delhi, his mind turned towards preservation.

It troubled him that the Qutb Minar lacked a top, so he had a stone pavilion specially designed in what he thought was an authentic period style and had it placed on the tower, surmounted in turn by a wooden canopy and a flagpole. From the outset this embellishment was controversial. Many people, from the governor general downwards, derided it, while Smith stoutly defended it. He pointed out that since no detailed records of the original survived, its appearance must be a matter of guesswork. Fair point, said his critics, but one thing we can be sure of: your guess is wrong. The traveller Fanny Parks compared the wooden canopy to a Chinese umbrella and was delighted when, during yet another storm, 'lightning struck it off, as if indignant at the profanation'. The stone part survived a little longer but was eventually dismantled in 1848. It was then reconstructed at the edge of the lawn to the south-east of the minar, where it remains today—a pretty but slightly forlorn and neglected little folly. With its fluted columns and curved *chajjas*, the pavilion's late-Mughal style might be deemed incongruous, but the criticism is pedantic because the construction of the minar has a long history, stretching beyond any one period.

Even without Smith's pavilion in place, the lofty grandeur of the Qutb Minar exceeds the expectations of most visitors. Emily Eden, the acerbic sister of Governor General Lord Auckland, developed a finely tuned style of put-down for most Indian things, but when she came to the Qutb Minar in 1838, she exclaimed, 'Well of all the things I ever saw, I think this is the finest.' She felt ashamed that she had not heard of it before and concluded, 'I do say it is rather a pity we were so ill taught.' As one of Delhi's finest landmarks, it does indeed deserve to be better known outside of India.

Back in the courtyard of the Quwwatu'l-Islam mosque—and featuring in one of Smith's paintings of the scene—is an object of greater antiquity. It predates the sultans, though it does perhaps tell us something about their ideas concerning power and history. It is an iron pillar, over twenty-three feet high, planted in front of the central arch of the prayer hall's screen. Its unblemished shaft is surmounted by a bulbous capital and other ribbed and fluted mouldings. An inscription in Sanskrit helpfully informs us that it is a standard of Vishnu, raised on Vishnupada hill by King Chandra. The first part is easily interpreted. A high pillar is sometimes raised as a standard in front of a Hindu temple to support an image of the vehicle of the god to whom the temple is dedicated. Such pillars are still common in Kerala, for example, where they are often plated in copper or brass. In this case, a neat hole in the top of the column shows where an image of Vishnu's vehicle—the eagle Garuda—was once attached. King Chandra has been identified as Chandragupta II (r. 375–413), making the pillar some 1600 years old—an age that causes metallurgists to marvel at the absence of rust. There is no agreement on where Vishnupada was, except that it was not in Delhi.

So this remarkable object is an imported antique, hauled to Delhi, according to bardic sources, by the Tomar Rajputs. Their veneration for it seemed to have impressed the early sultans who promptly appropriated it and set it up in the middle of their mosque. One may assume that the sultans did not see it as a standard of Vishnu, but they knew it was something old and special, and a symbol of reverence. And even though they were concerned to have their deeds recorded for posterity by wordy historians, they addressed the population around them by more visual means. Holding the column demonstrated authority.

That line of thought perhaps gave rise to the superstition that if you can stand with your back to the column, pass your arms around it and clasp your hands together, then you will live a long life. Parties of people laughing as they took their turn were once a common sight. But the pillar's current official custodian—the Archaeological Survey of India—has unsportingly erected a protective fence to stop this harmless custom.

Behind the ruined prayer hall, to the north-west, is the tomb of the second sultan, Iltutmish (d. 1236). The form of the tomb follows a type that had long been established in west Asia: a single square hall, with entrances on the south, east and north sides but closed on the west side by a mihrab: a niche that indicates the direction of Mecca. The hall was covered by a large dome which has collapsed—like the arches of the mosque screen, it would have been built on the trabeate system which is just not strong enough for a fully rounded dome on this scale. So the hall stands open to the sky. The sarcophagus, raised on a platform, occupies the centre of the building and is laid out on a north-south axis. The sarcophagus is visually very prominent—as one might expect—which makes it all the more surprising to realize that here (as is often though not always the case) it is empty; the sarcophagus you see is a dummy and the real one lies in an underground burial chamber directly below. The head of the staircase down to the lower chamber is located just outside the building, to the north.

The essentials of this arrangement—the domed square hall, the three openings, the mihrab, the orientation, the sarcophagus and the crypt—can all be found in earlier tombs in central and west Asia. An early prototype, for example, is the tomb of Ismail the Samanid at Bukhara (c. 900). This is in fact open on all four sides;

it has been suggested that it derives in turn from pre-Islamic fire temples. The fully developed form can be seen in the tomb of the Seljuq Sultan Sanjar at Merv (c. 1157). The builders of Iltutmish's tomb have clearly imported this ready-made type. Their successors in India were to retain all the essential components, even as they elaborated them into the most complex of forms. Sometimes the hall is octagonal rather than square, but all the other components are always there, whatever else is added. A single core concept links Iltutmish's tomb to the Taj Mahal built some four centuries later, and to every Muslim tomb in India in between.

What distinguishes Iltutmish's tomb from its west Asian sources is the profusion of rich ornament carved in stone over almost every surface. As in the mosque, the material and its treatment are the mark of the Indian craftsman's hand. The ornament mixes Quranic inscriptions with patterns, mouldings and motifs—like the lotus bud—that the masons were accustomed to using when carving temples.

Some other additions to the mosque—extensions to the courtyard and a new entrance to the south—date from the early fourteenth century, nearly a hundred years later (and are discussed in the next chapter). They show how the mosque founded by the first sultan continued in use for a long time under his successors. Indeed, despite the removal of the court to the other forts built by successive dynasties, the tomb of Imam Zamin, built in 1537 next to the Alai Darwaza, indicates that there was a resident imam here until the early Mughal period. After that the whole site seems to have become a graveyard, evident from the sheer number of graves all around, with some situated in places where they would be inconvenient for the people who came to pray, such as the central courtyard.

By the time Robert Smith and his critics came on the scene, the mosque had long ceased to be a place of active worship.

The presence of a small formal garden with a late-Mughal-style mosque, set aside near the modern entrance to the complex, suggests that by the eighteenth century the site had become just a place for members of the court to visit. They had need of a modern mosque while visiting an antique one because the antiquity could no longer be used, only seen. Many of the Mughal emperors from Babur onwards were avid architectural tourists. They visited historic monuments out of curiosity and to pass the time, much as we do today.

From the outset, the architecture of the Delhi Sultanate was an act of syncretism and assimilation. Similar things might be said about the Delhi sultans' approach to governance. Ethnically, they were Turkish (descended from tribes which had migrated into central Asia), but culturally they belonged to the wider Persian world, and they looked westwards for models of kingship. They assiduously read the classic Persian national epic, the Shah Nama, the 'book of kings'. They planned their courts on the Persian model, observing Persian customs and ceremonies, such as the celebration of Nowruz, the Persian new year. But at the same time they were tolerant, even respectful, of Hindu cultural traditions, and some Hindu festivals such as Holi, in spring, were also celebrated at court. They were operating in a terrain that was on the fringes of what they considered the civilized world and adapted themselves accordingly.

A case in point is their attitude to legitimacy. They had conquered a non-Muslim land by force of arms, but they made no attempt to convert the population forcibly. On the other hand, they sought to establish their right to rule by reference to authorities in the wider Muslim world. Qutb-ud-din, even while elevating himself to sultan, requested and received symbols of kingship, including the royal parasol, from the descendants of Muhammad of Ghur. His own successors went further, obtaining the necessary legal investiture from the Abbasid Caliphate in Baghdad. To regard themselves as kings they needed to know that they were seen as such within Islamic law, by the highest Muslim authority. But the day-to-day exercise of their power naturally meant interacting with many Indians who were not Muslims and including them in the administration. It would have been impossible, for example, to manage agriculture and taxation without local knowledge and support.

Qutb-ud-din made the transition from general to administrator with great dedication, and he was admired by contemporary chroniclers both for his piety and for his conspicuous generosity. His one diversion from work was *chaugan*—the precursor of polo—and it proved fatal: after serving just four years as sultan, he died in an accident while playing the game in Lahore.

He was succeeded by his son-in-law, Iltutmish (r. 1210–36), who seems to have been something of a mystic, much given to meditation and conversing with Sufi saints. But he did not neglect his duties, and considered the dispensing of justice the most important among them. Adopting a Persian custom, he ordered that anyone with a grievance should wear a particular dyed garment when attending court, so that on seeing him the sultan would immediately know there was some matter to be addressed. The famous Muslim historian and traveller Ibn Battuta adds:

> But he was not content with this. He said to himself, 'Some persons might be oppressed in the course of the night and might desire immediate redress of their grievances'. So he set up two statues of lions on towers at the gate of his palace, and around their necks were two iron chains with a huge bell. The oppressed person would shake the bell in the night and the sultan hearing the sound would instantly look into his case and administer justice.

The story might sound fanciful (and Ibn Battuta was reporting what he learnt a century after the events), but the idea of the ruler as a fair judge accessible to all—modelled on King Solomon—is a recurring motif in Islamic history.

Besides impromptu court hearings, Iltutmish found his sleep disturbed by numerous rebellions, staged by resurgent Rajputs or ambitious ministers. With an eye on posterity, he continued the building projects of Qutb-ud-din and paid particular attention to the education of his children. His eldest son predeceased him and was buried in a tomb, located near the modern housing colony of Vasant Kunj, known as Sultan Ghari which is again composed of the columns and lintels of an ancient temple. It was built around 1231 and was the first major mausoleum in Delhi.

This death left Iltutmish with a dilemma as he felt that his other sons, despite his efforts with their schooling, lacked the necessary qualities to rule, and he nominated his daughter, Raziya, as his successor. The nobles at first overruled him. When Iltutmish himself died in April 1236, they laid him to rest in the tomb next to the Quwwatu'l-Islam mosque and elevated his son Rukn-ud-din Firuz to the throne. As predicted by his father, Rukn-ud-din immediately abandoned himself to pleasures of the flesh. After seven months of forbearance, the nobles grew anxious for the safety of the realm and killed him, replacing him with Raziya.

The short reign of Raziya (1236–40) has been described by one historian as a 'bold experiment'. It was one of the few instances in Indian history of a woman ruling (and most of the others came much later). Early on she tried to maintain the conventions of purdah. Her throne was guarded by Amazons and surrounded by a screen, making her invisible to courtiers and public alike. But this proved impractical and she soon abandoned the attempt, switched to male clothing and rode about the city to transact business, thus setting a precedent that was imitated 600 years later by Sikander Begum of Bhopal.

Raziya controlled the administration and the competing factions at court much more satisfactorily than the three nonentities who followed her, each of whom was eventually killed by rivals. Their deaths cleared the way for the rise of Balban, a ruthless and ambitious courtier, to seize the throne.

Balban (r. 1266–87) began his life as a slave. There is a story that Iltutmish, given the chance to buy Balban, at first refused because he disliked his face, but was eventually persuaded by his wazir to give him a job in the stables. From there Balban worked his way up through various offices in the palace and postings in the provinces, emerging as the power behind the throne, finally usurping it. Because of his subservient beginnings—something he had in common with Qutb-ud-din—this whole succession of early sultans is traditionally referred to as the 'Slave Dynasty'. The term is something of an oxymoron, but it is a reminder that even while they appealed to external authorities to assert their legitimacy, they claimed no descent by blood from established ruling clans.

Feared rather than respected by fellow courtiers during the years of his rise to power, on account of his cunning and connivance, Balban adopted other methods once he had obtained his end. As sultan he developed a reputation instead for austerity and piety. He gave up alcohol, took to prayer with excessive zeal and closely supervised the political education of his sons. But he was still feared because of the harsh punishments he meted out to anyone suspected of sedition. In some cases entire villages were slaughtered.

The historian Isami records a tale about an elderly woman who came before Balban to plead for the life of her condemned son, insisting on his innocence. Balban ignored her pleas, and the young man was executed. Thereafter the woman appeared each night under the walls of the palace, loudly lamenting her loss and calling for divine retribution. All the efforts of the guards could not prevent the nightly repetition of her exasperating routine. But then, all of a sudden, one night she stopped coming. However, Balban's relief was short-lived, as he soon discovered that on that night his own favourite son, Prince Muhammad, had been killed in Multan. The woman could not be traced.

Balban was succeeded by his grandson, Kaiqubad. A handsome young man with pleasing manners, Kaiqubad had been brought up in accordance with his grandfather's strict regime and reached adulthood without ever having seen a woman or tasted wine. Predictably enough, once enthroned, he went berserk. He built himself a new palace which he filled with musicians, dancing girls and jokers. Members of the elite who shared his tastes joined in the non-stop revelry. Pliable members of the *ulema* (learned divines) were persuaded to write a fatwa exempting the sultan from fasting during Ramadan. He was distracted from pleasure only by the occasional need to murder a potential rival. It ended badly, of course, with Kaiqubad being wrapped in a blanket and thrown into the Yamuna river by the aggrieved son of someone he had killed.

Kaiqubad has no tomb and no trace remains of his pleasure palace. In fact, none of the palaces of these early sultans survive. The normal practice was for each ruler to construct a new palace, leaving those of their predecessors to decay. Their tombs, if built, were better maintained, because of the custom prevalent among later sultans of visiting the tombs of saints and of former rulers at important moments, such as before a military campaign. This custom seems to have been a matter of routine, causing some contemporary historians to comment on occasional lapses. We are told, for example, of a later sultan who refused to visit the tomb of Balban, suspecting him of having murdered his predecessor. If others shared his view, this might account for the dilapidated state of Balban's tomb by comparison with the well-preserved but older tomb of Iltutmish.

Of the greater part of the city of this time—the houses of nobles, merchants and craftsmen; their schools and markets—nothing substantial remains. Much of it would have been *kachha* (earth) rather than *pakka* (stone) in construction, made habitable by wooden and textile fittings, all of which was perishable. So when guidebooks point to the vicinity of the Qutb Minar as the first of seven Muslim cities of Delhi, they are really speaking of a fort that was wrested from the earlier Rajputs, containing a mosque composed of purloined pieces of temples and a few tombs.

Just outside the walls, abutting them on the south-west, lay a suburb, on the site of the present village of Mehrauli. Here too very little survives from the period of the first sultans. A large stone-lined tank, called the Hauz-i-Shamsi, is said to have been excavated around 1230 by Iltutmish in fulfilment of instructions personally delivered to him by the Prophet in a dream. But the tank today is much smaller than it was when Ibn Battuta saw it, and the stone has been replaced. At the north end of the village lies the dargah or shrine of the Sufi saint Khwaja Qutb-ud-din Bakhtiyar Kaki (known as Qutb Sahib for short). Born in Persia, he came to India soon after the conquest and became a disciple of Khwaja Muin-ud-din, the founder of the Chishti order in Ajmer. He died in 1236 (the same year as Iltutmish) so the nucleus of the dargah must date from then. But his original grave was covered by nothing but earth, in adherence with the general instructions for burial given in the Quran. The structure that now covers it, and the many other buildings within the complex, were all built by admirers and devotees at later times, some as recently as the twentieth century.

Expansion and Division: Khaljis and Tughluqs

After the death of Kaiqubad, order was restored to some degree when an Afghan noble of the Khalji clan usurped the throne. Though he had been a good general, he turned out to be a poor ruler, being far too lenient to command respect at court. He was especially indulgent towards his nephew Alauddin Khalji, who repaid the favour by assassinating his uncle in 1296 and taking his place.

This was not a popular move but Alauddin (r. 1296–1316) was not one to repeat his uncle's mistakes. He went to the opposite extreme in an attempt to monitor and regulate people's actions. In his regime the *muhtasibs* (censors of public morals) and *munihis* (intelligence officers) worked in concert to form a sort of secret police. They were especially severe on sexual crimes, drinking in public, narcotics, gambling and the hoarding of grain. All the prostitutes of Delhi were forced to get married. Alcoholics were imprisoned in specially made underground dungeons. 'All the roots of sin and crime are cut off,' bemoaned the poet Amir Khusrau. Even magicians were punished. Alauddin justified all this on religious grounds. According to one court historian, he admitted, 'If a man violates the wife of another, it does no harm to my kingdom. If a man drinks, I suffer no injury from it . . . [But] I do what the Prophet has commanded.'

It is unlikely that Amir Khusrau would have been impressed by that, as he once wrote, '*Kafir-e-ishqam musalmani mara darkaar neest* [I am an idolater of love, the Muslim creed I do not need].' One of the most famous Indian poets, he managed to retain an association with the Delhi court through several successive reigns and regimes. The focus of his thought, however, was not political but spiritual. He was a friend and devotee of the Sufi saint Nizamuddin Auliya, and composed numerous Sufi devotional hymns or qawwalis. He wrote in Persian but also in Hindavi, the local vernacular of the time (and among the precursors of modern Hindi). He also knew Sanskrit and incorporated Hindu ideas and imagery in his work. He is often pointed to as typical of the 'composite' culture of India under Muslim rule. It would be a mistake, though, to argue that the inclusive nature of his verse indicates a society that was free from religious divisions. On the contrary, we know those divisions existed precisely because Amir Khusrau was among those loudly berating them.

Though the best remembered and loved today, Amir Khusrau was not the only author or scholar at the court of Alauddin. There was, according to one modern historian, an 'unprecedented assemblage' of literary talent that the sultan promoted despite being himself entirely unlettered and 'an alien to the world of learning'.

The sultan's mind was focused not on verse but on expansion. Though careful not to leave the capital for long periods, he personally led numerous military campaigns in a quest to push back the frontiers of the empire, particularly towards the south. But the constant threat of rebellion kept a check on his ambitions. Early in his reign he moved his base to his army camp, situated at Siri, outside the city to the north-east. He had a protective stone wall erected around it, thus creating what has come to be called the second city of Delhi.

Much of this wall still stands and encloses, among other things, a sports complex, a residential colony (originally built to house athletes during the 1982 Asian Games) and the old urban village of Shahpur Jat, now overrun by restaurants and boutiques. There is also an auditorium where, from time to time, Delhiites gather to hear distinguished musicians sing the qawwalis of Amir Khusrau.

Alauddin's new city was serviced by a vast stone reservoir, the Hauz Khas, which was built outside its walls, to the west. Here too, on the bank, is an old urban village, similarly gentrified in recent decades by art galleries and fashion stores. The name Hauz Khas, though, is now applied more widely to cover the whole densely built-up region between the reservoir and the fort.

Alauddin did not neglect the old city. He planned a massive enlargement of the Quwwatu'l-Islam, the mosque built by his predecessors. Enlarging a mosque is technically a difficult thing to do, as it is essentially a courtyard enclosure whose boundaries are fixed. But with a steadily growing population the need was pressing since—notionally at least—the entire male Muslim population should be able to congregate for the Friday prayer. Confronted with the same problem earlier, Iltutmish had constructed secondary courtyards, like aisles, enclosing the first in its centre, thus providing more space for the faithful to assemble, on either side of the original core. Lest they feel excluded from the centre of action, the screen across the prayer hall was also extended, to run across the western ends of the new side courts. Alauddin's builders now proposed a further courtyard enclosure of such massive proportions that the existing parts would occupy merely one corner of it.

The Qutb Minar, which stands just inside the second courtyard, was also now deemed insufficiently grandiose. Alauddin proposed a second tower, with double the base area, that—in the words of an old guidebook—'was to have been double the height of the other, and yet perhaps not sufficiently high to represent his overweening pride'. The sultan reportedly employed 70,000 masons on these works. Even so, they were never finished. The rough rubble stump of the so-called Alai Minar in fact serves rather well to represent his thwarted ambitions. It is the architectural counterpart to his frustrated territorial campaigns. From time to time, the Archaeological Survey of India employs craftsmen to keep the buildings in good repair, and the outer courtyards of the ruined mosque echo to the chipping of masons' chisels, creating the illusion that descendants of the 70,000 are still frantically trying to complete the building of Alauddin's dream.

One part that he did complete—and it is worth all the rest—is the beautiful new entrance gate at the mosque's south-eastern corner, the Alai Darwaza. Faced with red sandstone and white marble panels, it is intricately carved both inside and out with a mixture of geometric and floral patterns. The dome, though not high on the exterior, is impressive when seen from within, and seems to be the first dome in India that was built (in 1310) on the true arcuate system. Adjoining the corresponding south-western corner of the mosque are the much plainer remains of a madrasa which is also believed to have been built by Alauddin. One building within this mini-complex is a tomb and is probably where Alauddin was buried when he died in 1316.

Alauddin was held in high esteem by later generations. His passing, though, must have been greeted with a sigh of relief in view of the strong-arm tactics and the ever-watchful eye of his police. His son and successor, Qutbuddin Mubarak Khalji (r. 1316–20) immediately relaxed all his father's regulations and set a different tenor to the court. Some accounts suggest that he liked to amuse his friends by dressing up and performing as a dancing girl. His favourite companion was a Hindu convert who went by the name of Khusrau Khan, by whom he was eventually murdered. Khusrau Khan, having flung the severed royal head from the roof of the palace, seized power and managed to retain it for some months. But his ban on cow slaughter made people doubt the sincerity of his conversion as well as his right to rule. The chaotic situation again invited a military coup, this time staged by a seasoned general named Ghiyas-ud-din Tughluq.

Having spent the larger part of his career until this point protecting the empire from the threat of Mongol invasion, Ghiyas-ud-din (r. 1320–25) enjoyed a high reputation for his valour, but was also considered unusually pious and compassionate for a military man. Contemporary chroniclers mention his friendship with saints and other religious leaders, his freedom from vice and his moderation in dealings with others. Ascending the throne does not appear to have changed him: he continued to receive praise for his respect for sharia (Islamic law) and his concern for the people's welfare. Of course it is not difficult or surprising to find praise for any sultan in contemporary sources, though in the case of really cruel or profligate rulers there is usually some dissenting voice. But views of Ghiyas-ud-din seem to be well summarized by the historian Barani who commented: 'Owing to Tughluq Shah's excessive justice and equity it was not possible for the wolf to look fiercely at the goat, and the tiger and the deer drank water at the same place.' The image of bestial harmony draws on familiar Islamic ideas, derived from a Judaeo-Christian tradition, about how the just monarch creates extraordinary peace and cooperation.

Opinions about his son and successor, Muhammad bin Tughluq (r. 1325–51) are more divided. According to some sources he had the same excellent character as his father. He was also erudite and a patron of scholars. He made his sisters and daughters marry religious men rather than members of the nobility. He abjured wine so strictly that it was simply not possible to buy it in Delhi during his reign. He did enjoy music and kept several hundred professional musicians at court, but nothing improper occurred at any of the concerts he hosted.

This picture of temperance and moderation is sadly contradicted by some of his actions. His reign got off to a bad start with the manner of the succession. Having personally commanded a campaign in Bengal, his father Ghiyas-ud-din was returning in triumph to Delhi. His son came out to meet him and staged an elaborate welcome ceremony a few miles to the south of the city. He invited his father and his brother (the presumed heir) to sit enthroned in a specially constructed pavilion, which promptly collapsed, crushing both occupants to death. Some insist that it was an accident, that the contrivance toppled over when some elephants, approaching to salute the sultan, trod on its steps. Others think that the pushing elephants were part of a plan.

Muhammad wasted no time in burying his father and assuming control. The tomb of Ghiyas-ud-din is a gem: neither large nor very ornate but perfectly proportioned. It stands within a miniature fortress, its dome and upper parts like a head and shoulders peeping over the battlements. The plain to its south was once a large artificial lake, created by a dam (now breached) so the composite fortress-tomb would originally have looked like a small island, or a ship afloat. To the north, overlooking and completing this picturesque composition, rise the craggy walls of Tughluqabad, a stupendous fort built by Ghiyas-ud-din that is reckoned as the third city of Delhi.

Tughluqabad is built over a rocky hill situated five miles to the east of the first city and the Qutb Minar. Its curtain walls on the southern side are up to fifty feet high and encase the hillside. Inside the walls, there are two further fortified areas: the small citadel in the centre of the south side, and a larger palace area covering the south-western portion of the fort. These two areas can be reached from one of the main entrance gates, which was also connected by a causeway to the tomb in its miniature fortress (the causeway has been severed by the modern road). The larger area within the walls, to the north and east, was the site of the city, containing the residential and commercial areas. Much of this part is now badly ruined, a mournful wilderness of rubble and scrub growth, though a modern village occupies one portion. The built-up part is also the home of Delhi's inland port. This is where cargo containers are brought (direct and still sealed from the docks of Mumbai) to be cleared through customs and assessed for tax. Here is a wilderness of a different kind, composed of rusting metal and oily puddles. It is enlivened by a storeroom with a display of luxury motor cars whose owners are unable or unwilling to pay the exorbitant import duty. Pigeons nest in them.

So it is hard now to get a sense of the original appearance of the place, or to connect what one sees with one of the few near-contemporary descriptions to survive—that of the traveller Ibn Battuta. He tells us that the bricks of the palace were plated with gold and that in the daylight 'they shone with such brightness and lustre that one could not gaze at it'. Perhaps he was exaggerating. After all, he also tells us that one of the tanks was filled not with water but with 'molten gold'.

The Tomb of Sultan Ghiyas-ud-din Tughluq, postcard by H.A. Mirza & Sons, c. 1910

Another seemingly miraculous feature of Tughluqabad is that the entire city, including the fort wall which is four miles in circuit, was all built in two years. This was achieved by the simple expedient of co-opting every available mason. While it was under construction, the Sufi saint Nizamuddin Auliya was in the process of building a large stepwell in the precincts of his hospice for the benefit of his followers. Ghiyas-ud-din ordered the workmen to abandon that work and concentrate on his fort. Reluctant to disobey the sultan but still devoted to the saint, they toiled on the fort all day and then sloped off to work on the stepwell by lamplight at night. So the sultan banned the sale of oil to the saint. Nizamuddin responded with a miracle and a curse. His workers found that their lamps burnt just as brightly with water. And Tughluqabad, said the saint, would only ever be inhabited by herders. It has certainly seemed that way in recent times.

Apparently it did not impress Ghiyas-ud-din's son Muhammad much either. At the start of his reign he embarked on two further large, and somewhat incompatible, building projects. He created Delhi's fourth city by enclosing the whole tract of land that lay between Siri (Alauddin's former camp) and the first Delhi. These two were originally quite distinct forts, separated by a distance of some four miles. Muhammad bin Tughluq constructed two long walls connecting them and enclosing the large area in between. This became known as Jahanpanah, the 'sanctuary of the world'.

Only a few short sections of these walls survive today and the buildings between them almost all date from later periods, so there is little to show for the fourth city. Even before it was finished, Muhammad bin Tughluq decided that the empire needed a second capital, in the south, to serve as a base for the expansion of that frontier. So he founded the new city of Daulatabad on the Deccan plateau (to the east of modern Mumbai). To accomplish this he had to move large numbers of masons to the south.

He also needed a population, and decreed that there would be a general migration. But he found that many of the citizens were reluctant to abandon the now developed comforts of Delhi to embark on an unpredictable adventure in the south, so they were slow to pack. The sultan's whole plan and the tactics he employed to coerce the populace betray the impractical whimsy and cruelty of a tyrant. When they refused to leave, he burnt their houses. Soldiers sent into one quarter of Delhi to see if anyone was hiding, still hoping to evade the removal, returned with two men, one blind and the other old. The blind man was fired from a catapult (though one assumes not as far as Daulatabad). The old man was tied by the leg to a trailer and was dragged all the way to Daulatabad. By the time the destination was reached nothing remained of him but the leg. Episodes like this account for the historian Ferishta's comment that Muhammad bin Tughluq 'seems to have laboured, with no contemptible abilities, to be detested by God, and feared and abhorred by all men'.

Daulatabad remained a strategic southern base for Delhi rulers for many generations, but Muhammad soon abandoned his experiment with the second city and everyone was allowed to return home. He later died while campaigning in Gujarat in 1351. All his efforts to expand the empire had proved futile. He was succeeded by his cousin, Firuz Shah Tughluq (r. 1351–88), who learnt the lesson of his predecessor's failure and concentrated his efforts on improving conditions in the existing domains.

Firuz Shah is described by contemporary historians as 'fair-complexioned, having a high nose and a long beard'. It is reported that he led a life of pleasure before unexpectedly coming to the throne, and then gave it all up. It is not clear, however, just exactly what he gave up. He continued to devote a lot of time to hunting, his favourite pursuit; indeed he built some fine hunting lodges. And despite numerous promises he failed to abstain from drinking wine. The change seems to have consisted largely in his taking a more orthodox attitude to law. To this end he introduced—perhaps for the first time in India—the tax known as *jiziya*, a levy that was commonly applied in the wider Muslim world on non-Muslim subjects. From this point on, over the ensuing three centuries, the periodic imposition or repeal of jiziya remained a controversial matter, in view of the predominantly Hindu population. The initial blow was softened in Firuz Shah's time by the simultaneous reduction in other taxes, and despite the divisive nature of the policy he remained a popular ruler.

He took great pride in the city, maintaining and adding to its fine buildings. When the top of the Qutb Minar was damaged by lightning he had it repaired, adding the upper two storeys which have white marble facing. The city at this time consisted of three contiguous large enclosures—the original Lal Kot, Jahanpanah and Siri—of which Jahanpanah, in the middle, was probably the least built-up. Tughluqabad, isolated to the east, lay largely abandoned, in fulfilment of the curse of the saint. But despite copious space for development within the existing forts, Firuz Shah was determined to build his own fortified palace complex on the bank of the Yamuna, far away to the north. Now known after him as Firuz Shah Kotla, this 'fifth city' substantially survives, though the new suburb that grew up around it, Firuzabad, has disappeared. What remains is the fortification wall that enclosed the palace and the Jami Masjid—a stately and handsomely proportioned mosque, undiminished in grandeur by its lack of ornament and partly ruined condition. Nearby is a stepwell with an unusual spiral inner staircase.

One of the embellishments of his palace is a so-called Ashokan pillar. This monolithic stone column, over forty feet high, bears an inscription on its smooth shaft composed by the Mauryan emperor Ashoka, in the third century BCE, to promote the Buddhist faith. Firuz Shah could not possibly have understood this. The script was first deciphered and the text translated by James Prinsep in 1837. But Firuz Shah evidently recognized it as something notable and—perhaps inspired by the earlier deployment of the iron pillar at the Quwwatu'l-Islam mosque—had it carefully conveyed all the way from its original location (Ambala, in Haryana) and erected on a specially made ziggurat in his palace. For good measure he brought another Ashokan column from Meerut and placed it on his hunting lodge on the northern ridge.

Firuz Shah's principal minister, Khan Jahan Junan Shah, was equally prodigious as a builder, claiming to have sponsored the construction of seven large mosques in Delhi (most if not all of which can be identified with certainty). The most remarkable of them, located back down south in what was then Jahanpanah, is the so-called Khirkhi Masjid or 'window mosque'. Though built of rubble, it is quite elaborately conceived. It rests, to begin with, on a high platform, so that each of the entrance gates on the north, east and south sides stands at the top of a flight of stairs. Once inside, you find that in addition to the covered prayer hall on the west side and the *liwan* (or cloister) running around the periphery on the other three sides, lines of columns supporting domes cross the centre of the courtyard, in both directions, bisecting each other. The net result is that instead of having a large open courtyard, there are four small open areas and the rest of the courtyard is covered and enclosed; hence the need for the *khirkhis* (windows) in the outer wall, to admit light and air. The arrangement is unusual. Something similar was attempted in another of the mosques—the Kalan Masjid in Nizamuddin—sponsored by the same minister, which raises the question whether it was a bit of experimentation with different possible permutations of the mosque form, or whether it was connected with a variation in function. Some large mosques accommodate a madrasa within their cloister. Covering part of the courtyard, and thus widening the cloisters, would make it possible to include a madrasa even when building on a smaller scale.

Expansion and Division: Khaljis and Tughluqs

Another appealing architectural project of Firuz Shah's reign, in which the sultan had a personal hand, was the madrasa built on the banks of Hauz Khas, the reservoir made earlier by Alauddin Khalji. It was established in 1352, at the very start of his reign, and soon became a major centre of learning. But it seems to have been admired as much for its buildings as for its scholarship. The historian Barani claims that 'its magnificence, architectural proportions and pleasant air make it unique among the great buildings of the world'. The poet Mutahhar of Kara was more lyrical:

> The moment I entered this blessed building through the gate, I saw an even space as wide as the plain of the world. The courtyard was soul-animating and its expanse was life-giving. Its dust was musk-scented, and its fragrance was like the odour of amber. There was verdure everywhere and hyacinths, basil, roses and tulips were blooming and were beautifully arranged as far as the human eye could see . . . Nightingales were singing their melodious songs everywhere.

The Madrasa at Hauz Khas, by an unknown photographer, 1890s

Even allowing for hyperbole, we may infer from this that expansive gardens once adjoined the buildings that we see today: an L-shaped complex overlooking the south-east corner of the (now much reduced) lake, with a courtyard behind.

These authors give few details of the curriculum of the madrasa, though Barani mentions *tafsir* (exegesis), hadith (the traditions of the Prophet) and fiqh (jurisprudence) as being among the subjects taught. It is quite possible that astronomy and medicine were also studied here. Barani was most concerned to stress that 'because this madrasa is a monument of good works and public benefaction, prayers obligatory and supererogatory are constantly being offered within its precincts'. Mutahhar was more interested in the menu in the dining hall, telling us that the students were fed on 'pheasants, partridges, herons, fish, roasted fowl and bulky kids, fried loaves and sweets of different kinds'. They drank pomegranate juice.

The structure at the corner of the complex is the sultan's own tomb. He had earlier built another tomb for himself elsewhere, in an area that is now a dense suburb near New Delhi Railway Station. That building incorporates a slab that is said to bear a footprint of the Prophet, specially brought from Mecca. But it was used for the burial of one of the sultan's sons, Fath Khan, who predeceased him. So Firuz Shah built himself a new tomb at this more restful location, amid the nightingales.

Chaos ensued after he died and was laid to rest here in 1388. Part of the problem was his longevity. He was over eighty, and there were members of three subsequent generations present to vie for the throne. His chosen nominee was a great-grandson but he was soon murdered, and the process began of working rapidly through the branches of the family tree. None survived very long and none exerted authority over the provinces, which were ruled by nobles.

A decade of instability in Delhi caught the attention of the Mongol warrior-ruler Timur, known to the Western world as Tamburlaine (derived from Timur-i-leng, meaning Timur 'the lame'). Taking advantage of the turmoil, he invaded India at the end of 1398 and sacked Delhi. For three days his army looted and destroyed the city. Like an old-fashioned invader, he was bent on plunder more than conquest. He hadn't really meant the citizens to be slaughtered, he said; they brought it on themselves by offering resistance. When it was over, he spent a fortnight relaxing at Hauz Khas—no doubt enjoying the excellent cuisine—and then set off to return to his capital, Samarkand, taking among his prisoners some of Delhi's finest architects and craftsmen.

Delhi was a wreck. The nominal sultan, Mahmud (a grandson of Firuz Shah) escaped to Kanauj, leaving a minister to try and restore order. He himself returned to Delhi only in 1405, and died there in 1412, the last of the Tughluqs.

Death in the Park: Sayyids and Lodis

Among the few groups in Delhi who were left unmolested by Timur were the Sayyids, members of families of Arab origin who claimed direct descent from the Prophet. As a Shia, Timur believed in the hereditary (rather than elected) succession of the caliphate and therefore held Sayyids in high esteem. One man in Delhi who claimed such a status was Khizr Khan. Modern historians doubt his claim (it seems highly unlikely that he was even Arab, never mind a Sayyid), but he appears to have persuaded enough of the right people at the time. In 1414, after the death of the last Tughluq, he seized the throne and ruled nominally as a deputy of Timur's descendants. Indeed he established a dynasty of four rulers, known as the Sayyids, which lasted for thirty-seven years until 1451.

This dynasty is generally written off. One historian refers to them derisively as people who 'called themselves sultans of Delhi'. Another asserts that they 'did not make any worthwhile contribution to the political or cultural life of medieval India'. The architectural historian Percy Brown, writing in the 1940s, noted that the Sayyids lacked the resources to build forts, cities, palaces and mosques on the scale of their predecessors and that all that survives of their work is their tombs. He then unfairly suggests that this was really a matter of choice: 'almost the only form of monument that appealed to the rulers and their subjects at this juncture, were those expressive of dissolution—they excelled in memorials to the dead'. Indeed they built so many tombs that Delhi 'was converted into a vast necropolis'. For good measure he adds that the Arabic word *maqbara*—used in India to mean cemetery or tomb-garden—is the source of the English word 'macabre'. He was wrong about that ('macabre' is derived from Old French), but his comments have been seized on by later writers wanting to depict the Sayyid era as a time of gloom and despondency.

In truth it was a time when the former empire was much diminished in size, its regional provinces having all broken away as independent states. Delhi was rather less important politically than the neighbouring sultanates of Jaunpur, Malwa and Gujarat, or the Rajput kingdom of Mewar. Putting a more positive gloss on this, one might say that the fifteenth century was a period when India's numerous regional states flourished to an unprecedented degree, politically and culturally. The centre meanwhile witnessed a series of palace coups and the ever-dwindling authority of the sultan. The second ruler of the dynasty, Mubarak Shah, was assassinated in 1434. The fourth and last of them bestowed on himself the regnal title Shah Alam (meaning 'King of the Universe'). Whether or not he intended to invite ridicule, he certainly received it. The standing joke was that 'from Delhi to Palam is the realm of Shah Alam'. Palam, later the site of the city's domestic airport, was then a village, five miles to the north-west of the Qutb Minar.

Even this was too much for Shah Alam to handle, plagued as he was by a duplicitous prime minister named Hamid Khan. In the end Shah Alam abdicated in favour of one of the nobles, Bahlul Lodi, who disposed of Hamid and—with the cooperation of other nobles whose confidence he won—slowly began to rebuild the empire.

Of Afghan descent and humble beginnings, Bahlul Lodi (r. 1451–89) took a pragmatic approach to governance, sharing power with loyal supporters and not insisting on the trappings of monarchy. Rather than using a throne, he sat on a carpet with the nobles and refused to allow any discrimination between himself and them or his former fellow officers in the army. He had a fixed daily routine, rising early, spending the morning on official business, the afternoon in the company of religious scholars and the evening in his harem.

After a reign of nearly forty years, he was succeeded by his son Sikander Lodi (r. 1489–1517) and grandson Ibrahim Lodi (r. 1517–26) who continued the process of reconquest and consolidation. Sikander seems to have kept up the austerity to some degree. One contemporary observer reports that he wore simple clothes and refused to wear new ones unless the old were torn. Ibrahim had a reputation for piety but, with a penchant for dancing girls and astrologers, was perhaps beginning to let things slide. There were always factions at court, and in the end one of these brought the Lodis down. They wrote to Babur, a descendant of Timur, to suggest that he might like to come to India and claim his rightful inheritance.

As with the Sayyids, no great forts or palaces are attributed to Lodi patronage. A few elegant mosques date from the later Lodi period, but mostly what survives are tombs—as pointed out by the merciless Percy Brown. In fact, tombs became even more numerous and conspicuous because the nobles built theirs as grandly as the sultans. The fine octagonal tomb of Sikander Lodi stands close to, and stylistically resembles, that of Muhammad Shah Sayyid. They compete for our attention in one of Delhi's finest parks, now known as the Lodi Gardens.

There are several layers to this space. There is evidence that it really was a garden in Lodi times (so the current name is perfectly just) but all trace of it vanished long ago, and by the nineteenth century it was the site of a village called Khairpur. When New Delhi was first laid out in the 1920s, the city stopped just short of the village, to the north; but in 1936 the poor villagers were evicted and the whole area was landscaped in English picturesque mode to create a London-style urban park, named (after the then vicereine) Lady Willingdon Park. Her name survives, carved in a stone gateway on the northern side. But only there. In the 1960s, Jawaharlal Nehru commissioned the architect Joseph Allen Stein to adjust the landscaping. The pond was added and the gardens were renamed after the Lodis, the original proprietors.

There is a puzzle about this place. If the picnickers, walkers, joggers and furtive lovers who make up the transient population of today's Lodi Gardens give little thought to scholarly disputes about its monuments, few would blame them. But the news that one of Delhi's sultans has generally been assigned to the wrong grave might cause them to pause momentarily.

A learned argument has long festered over the most central and conspicuous of the park's buildings, known as the Bara Gumbad. The question is whether it was originally intended as a tomb or as a gateway. The building's form alone does not supply an answer since formally sultanate gates and tombs are often similar: a big square box with arched openings surmounted by a dome. The Bara Gumbad clearly fits this general format, but which was it meant to be? Opponents of the gate theory pertinently ask: gateway into what? Being so large it is out of proportion as an entrance to the elaborately decorated but modestly sized mosque and the simple *mihman-khana* (guest hall) that are attached to it, one on either side; while it is well known that a mosque and a hall are often found near major tombs (a later example being the buildings flanking the Taj Mahal in Agra). So it must be a tomb. On the other hand, the argument against it being a tomb is simply that there is no grave, nor any evidence of there ever having been one. Both arguments seem sound. Stalemate.

As it happens, a solution was suggested many years ago by the scholar and antiquarian Simon Digby. In an article in an academic journal, he pointed out that before the whole area was re-landscaped to form a park in 1936, there was evidence that the Bara Gumbad had served as the entrance, not to the mosque, but to a large walled enclosure which included the further building now known as the Sheesh Gumbad. And this is the building we ought to be focusing on, because it is the tomb of Bahlul Lodi, the founder of the dynasty. Unmarked, unrecognized, noticed only for its flaking tile work, the Sheesh Gumbad turns out to be the nub of a whole complex dedicated to the first of the Lodis.

The Bara Gumbad in Lodi Gardens; photograph by the author, 1986

Anyone in Delhi who noticed this suggestion might have been surprised, because the Archaeological Survey of India has long designated a different building, situated in the dargah of a Sufi saint, in the suburb of Chiragh Delhi, as Bahlul Lodi's tomb. Digby's conviction that they have got the wrong building was based on a range of Mughal sources, the most convincing of which is a comment in Babur's memoirs where he records making a visit to the tombs of Sikander and Bahlul Lodi. It is important to note that Babur's memoirs were not composed by a court historian long after the events described, but a daily diary written by the emperor himself. So if he tells us that he spent a particular afternoon visiting two tombs, we may give it credence. The passage clearly implies that the two lie close together. There is no dispute about Sikander Lodi's tomb, one of the other monuments in the Lodi Gardens. It would be an odd sightseer's itinerary to start from there and then hotfoot it all the way down to Chiragh Delhi, south of Siri; but the easiest thing in the world to stroll across to the Sheesh Gumbad, a few hundred yards away.

A slightly later text, a history of Delhi's early sultans composed during the Sur period, mentions that Bahlul Lodi 'lies buried in his Jor Bagh'. The name means 'royal garden', and it tells us a great deal: in the first place that Bahlul Lodi was indeed buried in a garden not in a dargah; and secondly that it was indeed this very garden, because the name Jor Bagh survives even today as that of the housing colony on the south side of the modern Lodi Road, covering ground that was once part of the larger complex.

There's more. When Henry Sharp wrote a guidebook to Delhi in the late 1920s, the area of the gardens was still occupied by the village of Khairpur. He questioned the villagers about the historic monuments in their midst and found to his delight that they knew all about them. 'That one over there is Sikander's tomb,' they said confidently, 'and this one here, with the pompous great gateway, is Bahlul's.' Surprised by this evidence against the accepted version, Sharp went down to the dargah in Chiragh Delhi and asked the officials there about the building standing in the corner of their complex, the alleged tomb of Bahlul Lodi. 'Who?' they asked, blank-faced. 'Never heard of the fellow.'

Oral history and folk memory are usually treated with caution by professional historians, but in this case the testimony of the locals lends support to the evidence from literature, and from architecture. For the unimpressive building in Chiragh Delhi is anyway unconvincing, not being grand enough to serve as the resting place of the founder of a dynasty, even one with the egalitarian principles of Bahlul Lodi. It would be much more satisfactory to think of him lying in the elegant Sheesh Gumbad.

The mosque beside the Bara Gumbad contains some wonderfully intricate and remarkably well-preserved ornamental plasterwork and an inscription dating it to 1494. So, five years after the sultan's death, his tomb complex was finally complete, with the addition of the mosque, gate and guest house at the entrance.

Even if it is mistaken in the case of Bahlul Lodi, the notion that a sultan might be buried in the precincts of the dargah of a Sufi saint points to the prominent role played by Sufism in the religious and even political life of Delhi. The saint Nizamuddin Auliya (d. 1325) could count two sultans, Alauddin Khalji and Muhammad bin Tughluq, among his devotees. His relations with the intervening sultan, Ghiyas-ud-din Tughluq, were strained, and not just by that matter of the labourers and the oil; there is a suggestion that he was involved in the plot to assassinate Ghiyas-ud-din. As their teachings and reputations survived them, saints could win the devotion of sultans even after their passing. Firuz Shah Tughluq honoured the graves of both Nizamuddin and his pupil Nasiruddin Mahmud (d. 1356), known as Chiragh-i-Dihli (the 'Lamp of Delhi') after whom the district Chiragh Delhi is named.

The 'Lamp of Delhi' succeeded Nizamuddin as leader of the Chishti sect, an order that had been established in India by Muin-ud-din Chishti, whose dargah is in Ajmer, and was brought to Delhi by Qutb-ud-din Bakhtiyar (d. 1236), whose dargah is near the Qutb Minar. The teachings of these saints, as of other Sufis, are often described as representing the mystical or esoteric dimension of Islam. Sufism promotes turning the heart towards God and away from everything else; it teaches self-purification in order to achieve union with God, not after death but in life. Opinions differ, today and historically, on whether it can be considered orthodox. Its adherents insist that it is; that it involves no inconsistency or deviation from the teachings of the Prophet. But the question arises because, in the Indian context, Sufism does strikingly resemble bhakti, the form of Hindu devotion which similarly seeks personal union with the divine. The graves of some Sufis are even visited by Hindu pilgrims.

Sufism and bhakti have thus become linked in the public mind and in some religious practice despite the occasional efforts of hardliners to disentangle them. Such fusion is best embodied in the life and work of the poet Kabir (1440–1518). Though not a Delhiite, Kabir merits mention here as the most distinctive and cherished voice of his generation. A foundling of unknown parentage, he was brought up by Muslim weavers in the holy city of Varanasi, and later became a disciple of the Hindu saint Ramananda. His thought and poetry bridge the religious divide, vehemently opposing dogma to seek a common path. He acknowledged the existence of only two spiritual forces: God and the individual soul. The goal of life was to bring them into harmony.

Kabir was a contemporary of Sikander Lodi (d. 1517) whose tomb lies in the north-east corner of Lodi Gardens. Sikander's name is the Persian variant of Alexander—a reference to Alexander the Great whose history (or versions of it) had long formed a part of Persian literature, such as the account by the twelfth-century poet Nizami. A daunting name to live up to, and Sikander began by departing from his father's practice by getting up off the floor to sit on a throne and demanding displays of respect from his courtiers when they attended him in audience. His expansions and new foundations included the city of Agra as an alternative base to Delhi. Nothing of what he built there survives (having later been replaced by Akbar), and only the northern suburb of Sikandra still bears his name. Ironically, that district is now known chiefly as the burial place of Akbar, while Sikander himself is buried back here in Delhi.

His tomb marks an important step in the evolution of Indo-Islamic funerary architecture. At first glance, it is a replica of the much earlier tomb of Muhammad Shah (d. 1445) situated at the other end of the garden: like that, it follows the by now well-established octagonal variant of the type, with an enclosing veranda to encourage visitors to engage in a reverential circumambulation. The earliest tombs were square but there is nothing newfangled about the octagon. On the contrary, an octagonal-domed building within Islam cannot help but refer back all the way to the Dome of the Rock. Replicating significant aspects of the DNA, it establishes itself as a recognizable member of the family.

But the mutations are significant too. The elevated ground on which it stands is enclosed by a wall, making a garden. The much earlier tomb of Ghiyas–ud-din Tughluq (1325) stands in its own mini fortress, and Bahlul Lodi's tomb, as just discussed, was contained within a royal park and even had a compound wall; but Sikander Lodi's was the first Indo-Islamic tomb standing centrally in its own walled garden as an integral part of the architectural scheme. What its plan was, we don't know—only the bulbuls and parakeets flitting noisily among its flowers are unchanged from their ancestors—but its size and symmetry point to a formal design.

The garden wall allows for a second innovation. One of the challenges of tomb design, as already observed, is that the need to enclose the western side of the burial chamber—to accommodate a mihrab indicating the qibla or direction of prayer—spoils the symmetry, whether the plan is octagonal or square. But here the outer enclosing wall comes to the rescue. If you stand in the garden and look at the western side, you will observe a 'wall' mosque: an enormous arched mihrab inscribed over the wall, with a platform in front to accommodate those who assemble here for prayer. This does the job more than adequately, allowing the architect to leave the western side of the inner chamber open like the rest. The original idea is that the buried person's face can be turned towards the mihrab (and so to Mecca) within the chamber; in this variant, his gaze is directed through an open arch to the wall mosque beyond. The twist is that if you test this interpretation by going inside, you will find the western wall is not open at all but blocked. But look closely and you will notice that the infill is a much later addition. The western arch was designed to be open. Some later custodian of the building, clumsily misunderstanding the architect's intention, and pedantically asserting the rule so artfully evaded, has blocked it up and ruined the symmetry. Idiot!

In his classic survey of Indo-Islamic architecture, Percy Brown asserted—and many art historians have subsequently reiterated—that a third innovation here is the use of a 'double-shell' dome. It is a common practice in all domed architectural traditions to have separate inner and outer shells. A dome that creates a satisfying interior space, when seen from underneath, might be too shallow to be adequately imposing when seen from the ground outside; and the addition of a second shell over the top solves the problem. There are many such double domes in Indo-Islamic architecture. Humayun's tomb has one. In the case of the Taj Mahal, the void between the two domes is enormous. But in Sikander Lodi's tomb, the difference between the interior and exterior height is not obvious to the naked eye. Indeed, I am informed by a conservation engineer who was able to investigate the matter that there is none, or very little. Contrary to what we have repeatedly been told, it probably isn't a double-shell dome.

Close by is another monument of a very different kind: the so-called Aathpul, a bridge dating from the reign of Akbar. The 'aath' (eight) in its name refers (rather oddly, no?) to the number of piers rather than the number of arches, of which there are seven. It is a rare survivor of its type. As bridges serve an important practical function, most of those built in the Mughal era were later replaced by more modern constructions that can cope with modern traffic. This one survived because it lost its job. The nullah that it spanned, a small tributary of the Yamuna, was diverted before the modern era and the redundant bridge thereafter suffered neither use nor change. The absence of water, and a purpose, evidently bothered Joseph Allen Stein, the architect who refashioned the gardens in the 1960s: he introduced the pond so that the bridge had something to cross over. Only just, though. The bridge is right up against the eastern perimeter of the gardens, so there is not much space beyond it. Seen from the garden side, all appears fine: the vista of the pond terminates with the bridge under which the water flows. But if you stand on the bridge and look over the far side, there is not much to see but the swampy puddle that is the pond's other end. I'm not sure the pond makes the bridge any less of a folly; it is a bit like the bridge at the near end of the lake at Stourhead.

It does, however, carry the path that leads from one of the entry gates into the heart of the gardens. Midway along it is the last group of monuments at this site: a small mosque and the ornamental entrance to a rose garden, dating from the eighteenth century. Like the small mosque and garden of the same period located near the Qutb Minar, these buildings remind us that the later Mughal emperors, no less than their ancestors, liked to visit the monuments of the earlier sultans. They might even make a day of it, thus requiring a mosque for prayer and a garden for repose.

The loss of an empire does not improve anyone's resumé. The comparatively short reign of the last Lodi sultan, Ibrahim (r. 1517–26), terminated by the Mughal conquest, is inevitably projected as a story of decline and fall. This is to overlook at least one spectacular early success: in the first year of his reign he wrested control of Gwalior, one of the most powerful forts in central India, from the Tomar Rajputs. Many historians would be happy to overlook this, or not see it as a success, because it brought to an end the reign of Man Singh Tomar, among the most enlightened rulers and cultured patrons of his time. The court of Man Singh Tomar is famous still for its eclectic traditions of music and architecture, all brought to an abrupt closure by the loss of the powerhouse from which it emanated. Man Singh's son and successor, Vikramaditya, was dispossessed, and eventually died alongside his new overlord, trying to resist Babur's invasion at the Battle of Panipat in 1526.

In the meantime, Ibrahim Lodi, having neutralized one prominent Rajput ruler, was struggling to contain the expansionist ambitions of another: Rana Sanga of Mewar threatened Lodi control even over Agra, which lay far from his stronghold in

Chittor. Ibrahim also faced rebellion from within his nobility as rival factions of Afghan descent jostled for promotion and regional control. Some of those who failed to achieve it contacted Babur in a bid to remove Ibrahim from the throne. He was killed in the ensuing battle and was buried in Panipat in a structure that was hastily erected and is unsurprisingly un-majestic.

On the River: The Great Mughals

So strong is the association between Delhi's history and the Mughals that it is surprising to note that it got off to a slow start. The tomb of Humayun, the second ruler of the dynasty, is the city's finest historical monument, but Humayun himself spent very little time in the city where he lies buried. Neither did his immediate successors. Akbar and Jahangir were both constantly on the move, designating wherever they went as the capital; and if any city seemed to enjoy a status above the others it was Agra (which had been established as an alternative capital back in the time of Sikander Lodi and was rebuilt by Akbar). It was not until the mid-seventeenth century—the middle of the reign of the fifth Mughal emperor, Shah Jahan—that Delhi achieved its status as the undisputed capital of their empire. The founder of the dynasty, Babur, was a prince of distinguished lineage. He was descended on his mother's side from the rapacious Mongol known as Chengiz (popularly Genghis) Khan. The dynasty takes its name from this connection: 'Mughal' is a variant of 'Mongol', which is how they were seen by people in India. But Babur took greater pride in his paternal descent from Timur, who was famous not only for his ceaseless campaigns but also for his architectural embellishment of the city of Samarkand.

That city was the centre of Babur's cultural world and the focus of his early ambitions. Despite his illustrious, all-conquering ancestry, his inheritance was the small kingdom of Fergana (at the eastern end of present-day Uzbekistan). As a proud Timurid he yearned to recapture his ancestor's capital. He did, in fact, succeed three times in taking Samarkand, but he could never hold it for long and eventually conceded defeat and decided to look elsewhere for a kingdom. He began his migration southwards with the conquest of Kabul. From there, he made a series of forays eastwards as far as Lahore, but he was still not satisfied. Reminded (by malcontents at the court of Ibrahim Lodi) that Timur had also briefly conquered Delhi, Babur turned his sights in that direction.

Ibrahim Lodi was not ready to leave without a fight, simply out of respect for Babur's pedigree. Fortunately for Babur, he had, besides blood, some more persuasive advantages over the defender, including superior military tactics and gunpowder. His relatively small invading force—estimated at 15,000—was divided into highly mobile units and was backed by artillery. Ibrahim Lodi's defending horde, assembled on the plain at Panipat in April 1526, was outwitted and outgunned. Even his elephants, deployed to frighten the central Asians who were not familiar with the sight of them, were a failure, because they were themselves frightened by the unfamiliar noise of the artillery.

Babur's victory at Panipat decisively ejected the Lodis from Delhi, but his position was still precarious. He next had to subdue the even more considerable resistance of the Rajputs gathered under the central command of Rana Sanga of Mewar, whom Babur reckoned as one of the two most powerful of India's 'pagan' rulers. Only after he met and defeated this second force, at the Battle of Khanua in March 1527, could he consider the conquest accomplished.

Only then, too, could the new landlord pause to examine the property he had acquired. As he made his survey, his initial reaction was rather one of disappointment than of pleasure. Remembering his bewitching, ancestral Samarkand, he famously lamented in his diary that:

> Hindustan is a country of few charms. Its people have no good looks; of social intercourse, paying and receiving visits, there is none; of genius and capacity none; of manners none; in handicraft and work there is no form or symmetry, method or quality; there are no good horses, no good dogs, no grapes, musk-melons or first-rate fruits, no ice or cold water, no good bread or cooked foods in the bazaars, no hot baths, no colleges, no candles, torches or candlesticks.

There were some consolations, of course: 'Pleasant things in Hindustan are that it is a large country and has masses of gold and silver.'

Despite this brief, bitter outburst against India, Babur's writing more generally indicates a sensitive and inquiring mind. He was as much a poet and scholar as a soldier and statesman. His diary is one of the most engaging documents to survive from Mughal India, because it was written not by a professional stylist or flattering court historian, but by the emperor himself, for his own purposes. His aim was not to convey a sense of his majesty but to record his perceptions from day to day, and this he did with taste, humour, enthusiasm and occasionally with endearing artlessness. One of his chief interests was natural history. After giving an account of his conquest of India, he devoted a long passage to the country's flora and fauna. His description of the peacock is typically spontaneous, as if composed from notes made in the field:

> It is a beautifully coloured and splendid animal. Its form is not equal to its colouring. Its body may be as large as the crane's but it is not so tall. On the head of both cock and hen are 20 to 30 feathers rising some 2 or 3 inches high. The hen has neither colour nor beauty. The head of the cock has an iridescent collar; its neck is of a beautiful blue; below the neck, its back is painted in yellow, parrot-green, blue and violet colours. Below the back, as far as the tail tips, are flowers painted in the same colours. The tail of some peacocks grows to the length of a man's extended arms . . . Its flight is feebler [than] the pheasant's; it cannot do more than make one or two short flights.

Babur noted that, in Islamic law, it was permissible to eat peacock, but he felt an 'instinctive aversion' to the idea. His successors learnt that Hindus considered killing peacocks to be sacrilegious, so eating peacock was banned in Mughal India.

Despite his early dismissive comments on Indian handicraft, he soon came to rely on local workmen in his building projects. 'There are numberless artisans and workmen of every sort in Hindustan,' he remarked, noting that, '1,491 stone-cutters worked daily on my buildings in Agra, Sikri, Bayana, Dholpur, Gwalior and Kuil.' Some fragments of his work survive at these and other locations in his empire. But one place where he left no mark was Delhi. He had made a quick tour of inspection of the city in the days following the Battle of Panipat, visiting, as already noted, some of the tombs of earlier Delhi sultans. But then he hurried on to Agra and never returned. He died in 1530 and is buried, in accordance with his stated wish, at his earlier capital, Kabul.

The reign of his son and successor Humayun (r. 1530–40 and 1555–56) left greater physical traces on the city. The mosque and tomb of Jamali-Kamali, built on the outskirts of Mehrauli between 1528 and 1536, are among the earliest examples of Mughal architecture anywhere, and already show a surprising amount of refinement by comparison with the buildings of earlier dynasties. The façade of the prayer hall employs a restrained and clever use of colour coordination to articulate the parts and is elegantly proportioned. The small tomb in an adjacent enclosure looks nondescript from the outside, but the interior—the walls and the flat ceiling—is decorated with brilliant glazed tile work and cut and painted plaster. This exquisite gem is very little visited. Jamali was the pen-name of Shaikh Fazlu'llah, a poet and saint who flourished early in the reign of Humayun. Some of the verses inscribed on the walls are his. There are two graves (leaving very little spare space on the floor). Typically, neither is labelled and the second is traditionally said to be that of the poet's companion Kamali; but it is not known who this person was, and the name was obviously made up to rhyme with Jamali.

If poetry and architectural ornament were in safe hands in the 1530s, the empire was not. Even by comparison with his father's turbulent life, Humayun's career was unsatisfactory. A congenial but irresolute character, he temporarily lost control of the empire and nearly ended the Mughal dynasty as soon as it had begun. Aesthetic, nervous and clever, Humayun could on occasion exert himself with some success, but as often destroyed his own achievements through indecision or loss of interest. In 1540, he was dislodged from the throne by Sher Khan, a noble of Afghan descent who had established a power base in Bihar and Bengal, in eastern India. The usurper ruled from Delhi with the title Sher Shah, and was succeeded by his son Islam Shah. Having been forced to flee from India through the deserts of western Rajasthan, Humayun sought sanctuary in Persia. His road to recovery was long and arduous, but by 1555 (fifteen years after his eviction), the Sur interregnum was riddled with internal dissent, and Babur had gathered sufficient followers to enable him to return and recover his inheritance. And then within a year, he died.

Before the Sur revolt, Humayun had begun the construction of a new city of Delhi, its sixth. Situated to the south of number five, the Tughluq-era Firuz Shah Kotla, the new addition to the tally was named Din-panah ('the sanctuary of the faith') by Humayun. It included the handsome fort overlooking the Yamuna river, now known as the Purana Qila. The fort and a few buildings within it, completed by Sher Shah, are almost all that survives, though originally there was much more. The sixteenth-century Jesuit, Father Antonio Monserrate, notes the mansions and gardens that clustered around the fort in his time; which in turn were protected by a city wall that has now disappeared, leaving only the northern and western gates as isolated structures.

The northern gate—which stands in the middle of the modern main road just outside the Kotla—was originally called the Kabuli Gate, following the normal practice of naming gates after a distant city towards which it faces. But it is popularly known as the Khuni Darwaza (or 'bloody gate') because, according to one version of events, it was here that two sons and a grandson of the last Mughal emperor, Bahadur Shah Zafar, were shot dead in cold blood in 1857. Having been arrested at Humayun's tomb (to the south), they were being escorted back to Shahjahanabad (to the north); but fearing they might try and escape, their escort, Captain Hodson, changed his plan and executed them summarily in the middle of their journey.

By that date little remained of the early Mughal city that once stood here. The view of the area made by Thomas and William Daniell in 1789 and later published in their series *Oriental Scenery* may be exaggerated in respect of the uneven torn-up terrain, but it shows hardly anything outside the fort walls. A little later, the Purana Qila became a favourite haunt of Robert Smith, the engineer who put a cupola on the Qutb Minar.

Part of the moat survives and has been turned into a boating lake. The dilapidated northern entrance gate of the fort, towering above this, still presents a decidedly picturesque image, but it is the sturdier western gate that now serves as the main entrance. Inside the fort is the exquisitely detailed Qila-i-Kuhna Masjid, a mosque built by Sher Shah Sur in 1541, which is decorated with elaborate carving and panels of inlaid stones. The five arched entrances into the prayer hall are of different sizes, the central one being the highest. Each is contained within a larger arched recess, which again are assorted in size, creating an agitated formal rhythm across the façade that is enlivened by the carved ornament.

The two men who built this fort could not have been more different in temperament. The intellectual Humayun was fascinated by astrology and employed it to organize his administration. For example, he attended to matters of a given kind only on days that were governed by a suitably symbolic planet. The system was no doubt elegant but it was not always efficient or responsive to emergencies. Central authority began to drift. Sher Shah was the grandson of an Afghan adventurer who had come to India and taken service under the sultans; but not content with such a position, the grandson established an independent power base in eastern India. When he detected that the centre was weakened by Humayun's eccentricity (and by the disloyalty of his brothers, it should be added), he seized his chance and usurped the throne. A pragmatist, he swept aside Humayun's astrological conceits and implemented sound systems of government. His reform of the tax revenue and his programme of road building were measures that anticipated and facilitated the more extensive reforms later undertaken by

Akbar. In hindsight, because of the return to Mughal rule, the Sur interregnum looks like a blip and historians generally give the credit for building the empire to Akbar. But the biographers of Sher Shah make a good case for allotting at least part of the credit to him. Readers of Kipling might have noticed that the tiger in *The Jungle Book* shares the earlier form of his name, Sher Khan, and this is only in part because his name does actually mean 'tiger'; it is also because of his reputation for ruthless cunning.

It is not clear whether Humayun or Sher Shah were aware that the land they were building on was identified by some as Indraprastha, the ancient city of the Mahabharata. One of them (it is not clear which) dug a stepwell in the fort, but not being archaeologists they did not preserve any painted greyware that they might have found in the process. The potsherds and other ancient artefacts that were excavated in modern times are displayed in a small museum at the site.

Close to the mosque stands a large octagonal pavilion known as the Sher Mandal. The name implies that this too was the work of Sher Shah, but some experts date it later on stylistic grounds, without explaining who would have built here at a later date and why. Humayun would scarcely have had time, between his return from exile and his death, to erect even this relatively modest structure. But if it was already there, as is commonly believed, he would have certainly appreciated it. During his enforced exile in Persia, Humayun had developed a great liking for Persian painting, and on his return to India he brought with him two master artists to help establish the Mughal atelier. The two-storeyed octagonal Sher Mandal resembles the pleasure pavilions so often depicted in Persian art, at least in form though not in materials since it is made not of painted wood but of blocks of sandstone. If the traditional but unconfirmed story is to be believed, Humayun discovered the difference the hard way. It is said that he used the building as his library and accidentally fell down its stone staircase, sustaining the injuries from which he died.

The tomb in which Humayun lies buried took fifteen years to construct (1556–71) and marks the true beginning of Mughal architecture on the grand scale. Traditional scholarship attributes the commissioning of the building to the emperor's grieving widow, Hajji Begam, but this is a pious fiction that disguises its true meaning and purpose. Such a magnificent building was clearly meant as a statement of power and of permanence, and as such could only have been commissioned by the new emperor, the young Akbar (r. 1556–1605). It addressed the people of Delhi and assured them that, despite appearances to the contrary, the Mughals were here to stay. At the time, some people in Delhi might have been anxious on this score. Anyone born just before the conquest had seen such change that it must have left them reeling in dizziness. First the Mughals come and knock out the Lodis; then the Surs come and knock out the Mughals; then the Mughals come back and knock out the Surs; and now the emperor falls downstairs and is succeeded by a teenager. Perhaps the Surs will stage a comeback. The lofty dome of Humayun's tomb lays all such fears to rest along with the late emperor. Pushovers don't build like this.

If it was indeed intended as a monument not just to Humayun but to the Mughal dynasty, then it is fitting that so many other members of the imperial family—princes and princesses of later generations—lie buried here too. Their graves are scattered in the rooms that surround the central hall, on the terrace, and in the alcoves of the basement. Humayun's tomb was also the scene where the last chapter of the Mughal era was played out nearly 300 years after its completion. The last emperor, Bahadur Shah Zafar (r. 1837–57), the reluctant figurehead of the rebellion against British rule in 1857, sought sanctuary here after the fall of Delhi, and was here arrested by the ruthless Captain Hodson.

The design of the tomb is usually attributed to a Persian architect named Mirak Mirza Ghiyas. His nationality might mislead us. Some of the design's more obvious Persian features, such as the plan of the garden and the disposal of halls around the central chamber, are things that had already been introduced into India earlier. In the scale and form of the main arches and domes, the architect appears to have drawn inspiration more particularly from the buildings of Samarkand, the city (in modern-day Uzbekistan) that had served as Timur's capital. And this no doubt reflects the wishes of the patron, for the Mughals identified themselves as Timurids: that was the lineage they were most proud of.

Humayun's tomb, by an unknown photographer, c. 1870

But if, while erecting a monument that would declare the power and permanent presence of their dynasty, they chose to advertise their foreign origins, the building no less emphatically declares its Indian location and identity. For one thing, it is faced with finely finished sandstone, quarried in the region to the west of Agra, and detailed with carved ornament that reveals the Indian mason's hand. Central Asian buildings are often built of rubble and faced with glazed tiles. In the Indian adaptation of that method, the tiles were often replaced by dressed stone, as both the material and the skills to work it were abundantly available. Not everyone was impressed. This technique caused Edwin Lutyens to describe Mughal architecture as 'veneered joinery in stone'.

Humayun's tomb, built in the 1560s, was the first in a sequence of magnificent Mughal mausolea that place the tomb structure in a *char bagh* or Persian paradise garden. The restoration of the garden and its waterworks was carried out in the opening years of this century as a gift to India from the Aga Khan, in celebration of fifty years of India's independence. Work on the main structure is also now underway.

The interior is grand but solemn, and disappointing to some, after the colours of the stonework and the garden. Having mounted the podium, one enters from the south portal. This is the usual arrangement with all such tombs. Also as usual, the body is interred on a north-south axis, with the head in the north, and the visitor approaches at the feet. As previously observed, the western side of many tombs is enclosed to accommodate a mihrab or niche that indicates the qibla (the direction of Mecca). But here the architect was seemingly reluctant to disrupt the building's symmetry and has left the west side open, at least to light and air, for the arch is filled by a jali or perforated screen, like the corresponding arches to the north and east. But then, in an ingenious innovation, the outline of a mihrab is superimposed over the western jali, so the convention is respected after all.

The central hall is octagonal. On the three sides that face west, north and east, as noted, there is a large arch with a jali. On each of the four sides that do not face a cardinal direction, a door leads through to a further hall, which houses further graves. So, four large octagonal blocks surround a central one, attached to its 'odd' corners, and are sufficiently fused together to make the overall plan almost a square. In the spaces between them on the 'even' sides there is a huge scooped-out arch, or *iwan*, that penetrates from the outer façade to the edge of the inner hall. Except on the south side, where the corresponding space is enclosed by a flat wall, to make an entrance hall. Stepping back out, you will notice that the southern façade differs from all the others. Where the entrance.

The southern entrance in this case is a little disorientating because one enters the garden from its western gate. Originally the main garden gate must have been the one on the southern side, which is now crowded round by a modern housing estate. The western gate serves as the present entrance because of its proximity to the Mathura Road. On that side too lie the remains of an older enclosure, known as Bu Halima's garden, though it's not known who that noblewoman was. She is not the only neighbour. There are numerous other tombs in the vicinity, with occupants known or unknown. The so-called barber's tomb stands inside the garden, in the south-eastern corner; the Nila Gumbad ('blue dome') is just outside to the east, near the modern railway line; and the Sabz Burj ('green tower') occupies the roundabout on the Mathura Road.

Adjoining Bu Halima's garden to the south is a large octagonal enclosure containing a tomb and a mosque built in

1547 for Isa Khan, a noble at the court of Sher Shah Sur. The tomb is also octagonal and almost identical to those built in that form during the Sayyid and Lodi periods. Adjacent to the east and extending up to the wall around Humayun's tomb is another spacious enclosure known as the Arab Sarai. This was originally intended as a caravanserai, a resting place for travelling merchants and pilgrims, but was partly taken over by yet another mosque and tomb complex, known as Afsarwala and built for another sixteenth-century noble. The sturdy Archaeological Survey notice informs us that the incumbent is an unidentified commander and that the name is derived from the English word 'officer'. So it is the 'officer-wala's tomb'. They do not explain why anybody at the Delhi court would adopt and corrupt an English word as early as the sixteenth century, a time when most military vocabulary was derived from Turkish. But some painstaking research by the historian Subhash Parihar reveals that Afsar was a Persian tribal name, and that there were several Afsars employed at the early Mughal court, including one who assisted Humayun during his victorious return and recapture of India in 1555. So he is a likely candidate for the patronage of these two elegant structures, placed near the tomb of his former master. So yes, fair enough, he was an officer. But Afsar was his name.

Even Humayun is not the lead character in this neighbourhood of the dead. The area developed into a necropolis (with many subsidiary burials within the established tomb gardens) because of its proximity to the dargah of the Sufi saint Nizamuddin Auliya. The idea was that, when the dead are raised on the Day of Judgment, those who have lain so long in the earth close to a saint, whose ticket is guaranteed, might benefit as he will speak up for his close companions.

These days the busy Mathura Road separates Humayun's and the other garden tombs from the grave of the saint, embedded in the dense urban village named after him as Nizamuddin. But having toured the carefully preserved monuments and manicured lawns on one side of the road, it is worth stepping across to visit a tomb that is still a living sacred site, a place of continuous pilgrimage, of avid worship and haunting music. Some of the qawwalis you might hear there were composed by the poet Amir Khusrau, a friend and contemporary of the saint, who is also buried near his mentor in the precincts. A much later follower of the saint's teachings, the seventeenth-century Mughal princess Jahanara, is also to be found here. The loyal daughter of Shah Jahan and his queen Mumtaz Mahal, who is buried in the Taj Mahal, Jahanara has a touchingly simple grave in a modest if elegant enclosure. The scooped-out top of the sarcophagus is designed to facilitate the planting of grass or flowers, in compliance with the orthodox notion that nothing but earth should cover the grave of the faithful.

Having set his mark on the city of the sultans, in the form of his father's tomb, Akbar moved on to Agra and rarely revisited the old capital. Throughout his long reign, which spans the second half of the sixteenth century, Akbar was always on the move, commanding campaigns, suppressing revolts and forging alliances. The empire that had been formed by the Khaljis and the Tughluqs in the fourteenth century lay fragmented after Timur's invasion. Akbar's outstanding military achievement was that he reunited the whole of north India (down to a line running from Mumbai to Puri) under Mughal rule. Independent sultanates like Malwa and Gujarat that had broken away were brought back under central control. The Rajput states were subdued, sometimes by force (as in the siege of Chittor in 1567) but more often by carefully balanced strategic alliances. Many members of the ruling Rajput families—maharajas and their sons—were encouraged to join the imperial service as commanders and regional governors. By this means, and by marrying Rajput princesses, Akbar succeeded in converting the greatest potential internal threat to his empire into its strongest support.

Akbar frequently shifted his base according to the pressing needs of the moment. He rebuilt the forts of Agra, Allahabad and Lahore, well placed for dealing, respectively, with central and eastern India and the northern frontier. The one phase of his reign when he seemed more settled—in the 1570s—was when he built the palace complex at Fatehpur Sikri. Delhi was not his home.

It remained home, though, for some people who were close to him. One such was Maham Anga, his former wet-nurse. More than a mother figure, Maham Anga was a shrewd political fixer in the early years of Akbar's reign, who used her influence over the young emperor to frustrate the ambitions of her rivals. Her most conspicuous victim was Bairam Khan, the loyal general who led all of Akbar's major campaigns in the opening years of the reign but was dismissed from service, on Maham Anga's advice, in 1560. With Bairam Khan out of the way, Maham Anga was able to advance her son, Adham Khan, who had been Akbar's childhood playmate. This impetuous youth was not up to the roles assigned to him. In a fit of jealousy, he murdered a senior official, Ataga Khan (the husband of another former wet-nurse). Akbar ran into Adham Khan as he was returning from the deed, and disarmed the fleeing assassin by punching him in the face. He then ordered the unconscious Adham to be thrown from the parapet. Surprisingly the fall did not kill him. So Akbar ordered him to be carried up and thrown again, until he was dead. He is buried in a large and handsome tomb close to the walls of the Lal Kot in Mehrauli, next to a stinking garbage tip. It is built on an octagonal plan, a throwback to a design that had been adopted for some tombs of the Sayyid, Lodi and Sur eras. It is popularly known as the 'Bhul-bhulaiyon' or maze, on account of the complicated internal corridors in its upper level. Adham Khan's victim, Ataga Khan, is buried in a gem of a tomb close to the dargah of Nizamuddin Auliya. Smaller, and built on a square plan, it is more compact and has exquisite inlay work over its external surfaces.

Another octagonal tomb of this period, also in Mehrauli but closer to the Qutb Minar, is that of Adham Khan's brother, Quli Khan. This building is exceptional because in the early nineteenth century the governor general's agent in Delhi, Thomas Metcalfe, bought it from Quli Khan's descendants and converted it into his summer house. He named it 'Dilkusha' or 'heart delighting'. Metcalfe's main residence, like those of other British officials of his time, lay to the north of Shahjahanabad, as far away as one could get from this spot. He came here either for the peace and quiet or to stay close to the emperor of his day, Bahadur Shah Zafar, who also had a house in Mehrauli. Metcalfe lived in Delhi for forty years (1813–53) and was one of the 'White Mughals'—those early British residents who readily adopted Indian customs. And Dilkusha is a cultural hybrid: a Muslim tomb converted into an Englishman's house set amid picturesque gardens and scattered purpose-built follies. There is even a little lake and a boathouse, and the local village boys come to play cricket on the lawn. You can easily imagine yourself in the English Home Counties, but for the ruined Akbar-period arches overhead.

The reign of Akbar's son Jahangir (r. 1605–27), considered from a Delhi perspective, is similarly marked by the absence of the emperor from the city and the construction of a couple of notable tombs. One of them is a white marble pavilion, enclosed by pierced screens, with a flat roof supported by sixty-four columns (from which it takes its popular name, Chaunsath Khamba). The form is unusual but in one sense more orthodox than the domed tombs, because Islamic law prescribes simple enclosures rather than grand sepulchres for burial. It is situated not far from Ataga Khan's tomb and the principal occupant is his son, Mirza Aziz Kokaltash. When his father was murdered, he was appointed in his place and flourished under Akbar's patronage. His relations with Jahangir were less stable (he spent a period out of favour and in jail), but he lived to the age of eighty-five.

Further south, on the other side of the busy Mathura Road, stands the tomb of another famous son: Abdur Rahim Khan, usually referred to by his title, Khan-i-Khanan. His father, Bairam Khan, was assassinated when he was a small child, but he grew up in court circles and eventually more or less took his father's former place as a devoted and reliable servant of Akbar. He continued in service under Jahangir but had a more difficult time with him. At one point, suspected of disloyalty, he was sent his son's severed head, which was served to him like a melon. The Khan-i-Khanan was a man of considerable learning who patronized poets and wrote himself, in Arabic, Persian and Hindi, under the pen-name Rahim. His once grand tomb follows the pattern of Humayun's in style: it is smaller and more compact, and squarer in overall form. According to his latest biographer, he built it originally for his wife, Mah Banu; certainly, both she and he are buried in it. It is much diminished by the loss of the marble cladding on the dome—allegedly stolen in the eighteenth century by a prime minister who wanted it for his own tomb.

During the years of his reign, Jahangir divided his time between various centres. These included Agra, from where he supervised the building of Akbar's tomb in the suburb called Sikandra; Ajmer, where he was met by Sir Thomas Roe, the first ambassador sent by Britain to the Mughal court; Kashmir, where he exercised his passion for garden design; and Mandu, the sprawling fort at the heart of Malwa. Delhi, by contrast, began to show signs of neglect. Two early British visitors, passing through in 1615, noted that 'the inhabitants are poor and beggarly, by reason of the king's long absence'.

Matters did not immediately improve under his successor, Shah Jahan (r. 1627–58). Initially preoccupied with the wars in the Deccan, Shah Jahan established his base at Burhanpur. He also spent much time in Agra. In the course of the 1630s he replaced many of Akbar's sandstone palaces within the Agra fort with a suite of white marble apartments for his own use. At the same time he also supervised the building of the Taj Mahal on the riverbank at Agra, the tomb of his favourite wife, Arjumand Banu Begam, known as Mumtaz Mahal.

Then in 1638 Shah Jahan took the bold decision to re-establish Delhi as the capital of the empire. Bold because, rather than occupying or developing any of the numerous existing citadels, his plan involved starting again from scratch, building an entirely new city (counted the last on the traditional list of Delhi's 'seven cities') on a site to the north of the previous ones, on an unprecedented scale. It even had a new name. Though often referred to as Delhi in both historical and modern sources, it is officially called Shahjahanabad, after its founder.

The principal buildings and streets were laid out over the course of ten years and were ready for occupation by 1648. First came the fort, called the Lal Qila or Red Fort, containing the imperial palace and the headquarters of the army. This was located to the east, on the bank of the Yamuna river, thus replicating the arrangement in Agra, though on a more orderly plan and a much larger scale. This position also abuts the Salimgarh, a fortified enclosure that had been built during the Sur interregnum and was one of the few previously existing buildings on the site. Though surrounded by a moat, the fort was connected to the city that grew up on the designated space to its west and south by two great arterial roads. One of these roads, now known as Chandni Chowk, ran east-west, from the main gate of the fort, right across the whole breadth of the city. The second, Faiz Bazaar, ran from the fort's southern gate to the city's southern perimeter. On an elevated rock situated on the angle between these two perpendicular roads, Shah Jahan built the Jami Masjid, the new city's congregational mosque, the largest in India.

Finally, the whole city, covering a space of two and a half square miles, was surrounded by a wall. Unlike the handsome, dressed sandstone walls of the Red Fort, the city wall was originally made of a mixture of rubble and mud, held together by cement. Only the gates were built of stone. Much later, in the early nineteenth century, parts of the wall were reinforced and rebuilt in stone by the British, though the only people kept out by this work were the British themselves, in 1857. Nowadays, most of the city wall has disappeared, though one portion survives on the eastern side, to the south of the Red Fort. As modern roads now run immediately outside where the wall once stood, the original shape of the city is preserved on the map. And the gates on the southern side still stand, so that while approaching the city one has at least the illusion of entering a walled city, and it is still commonly described as such, though in fact it has ceased to be one.

Much has changed inside the non-existent walls too. Old Delhi—as it is now called—certainly has a vitality of its own. Its narrow lanes and congested markets are effervescent with commerce and life. But the grandeur of an imperial city has largely evaporated. Even the space immediately around the fort, though more open and uncluttered, is not maintained with any sense of history. The police barricades, the symbolic and tedious security system (increased in response to a terrorist attack in 2000), and the great swathe of grey tarmac, do little to enhance the fort's splendour.

To get a picture of how it once was, we may turn to a description written in 1663 by François Bernier, a French physician who lived in Delhi. Bernier tells us first that the broad strip of sandy ground between the Red Fort's eastern wall and the river was used for staging elephant fights and for military reviews for the benefit of the emperor, 'who witnesses the spectacle from the windows of the palace'. Today a rather feeble formal garden occupies this space, but many Delhiites will recall the days when it was the site of the Chor Bazaar (or 'thieves' market')—a lively place that specialized in goods of dubious provenance and authenticity. The river moved away long ago: broad but shallow, it was always liable to change and has shifted its course to a more easterly line.

On the western side of the fort, facing towards the city, Bernier tells us there was 'a deep ditch faced with hewn stone, filled with water, and stocked with fish'. The ditch was connected to the river, the likely source of the fish. It is hard to imagine anything living in the polluted waters of the Yamuna today. Bernier next describes the area that is now smothered in asphalt:

> Adjoining the ditch is a large garden, filled at all times with flowers and green shrubs, which, contrasted with the stupendous red walls, produce a beautiful effect. Next to the garden is the great royal square, faced on one side by the gates of the fortress, and on the opposite side of which terminate the two most considerable streets of the city. The tents of such Rajas as are in the king's pay, and whose weekly turn it is to mount guard, are pitched in this square . . . In this place also at break of day they exercise the royal horses, which are kept in a spacious stable not far distant; and here the Kobat-khan, or grand Muster-master

of the cavalry, examines carefully the horses of those who have been received into the service . . . Here too is held a bazaar or market for an endless variety of things; which like the Pont-neuf at Paris, is the rendezvous for all sorts of mountebanks and jugglers.

Perhaps the old Chor Bazaar was not so inauthentic after all. But in complaining of 'mountebanks', Bernier had his sights on the astrologers, whom he regarded as peddlers of superstition:

These wise doctors remain seated in the sun, on a dusty piece of carpet, handling some old mathematical instruments, and having open before them a large book which represents the signs of the zodiac . . . They tell a poor person his fortune for a *paysa* (which is worth about one sol); and after examining the hand and face of the applicant, turning over the leaves of the large book, and pretending to make certain calculations, these impostors decide upon the *Sahet* or propitious moment of commencing the business he may have in hand. Silly women . . . flock to the astrologers, whisper to them all the transactions of their lives, and disclose every secret with no more reserve than is practised by a scrupulous penitent in the presence of her confessor.

No less a piece of theatre—though vastly grander and more architectural—is the fort itself and the imperial palace complex within. Though no doubt meant to house and to protect, it is also designed to awe, to make us cower in submission. Its grand west entrance, the Lahore Gate, is visible from the entire length of Chandni Chowk, the city's main arterial road even today, despite the traffic and accretions, and must have been even more imposing when the view was less impeded.

Chandni Chowk; photograph by Samuel Bourne, 1865

The barbican that curls in front of Lahore Gate, somewhat diminishing its impact as we approach, was added by Aurangzeb. It is traditionally believed that Shah Jahan, who lived to see it (or at least hear about it), was dismayed and complained that his son had added a superfluous veil. And if the story is true, it is evidence that the fort's creator was thinking more in visual than in military terms. Entering the gate, we are immediately plunged into the dimness of the Chatta Chowk, a tunnel of market stalls, originally stocked with provisions for the palace's residents, now piled high with the usual tourist curios.

We emerge into a sunlit space that was once an enclosed square and a crossroads. Level with this point a broad street ran from left to right across the whole width of the fort, down to the Delhi Gate on the southern side. Looming on our left are the British barracks that saddened the heart of the architectural historian James Fergusson, but which are now restored and cherished as relics of one period of the fort's history. Straight ahead stands a stately red sandstone pavilion known as the Naqqar Khana, after the drummers' chamber that was housed in its upper storey. A common feature in Indian palaces, a *naqqar khana* was where musicians assembled to help proclaim arrivals and departures and to signal the passing phases of the day. François Bernier found the sound hard to get used to:

> To the ears of an European recently arrived, this music sounds very strangely for there are ten or twelve hautboys, and as many cymbals, which play together . . . On my first arrival it stunned me so as to be insupportable: but such is the power of habit that this same noise is now heard by me with pleasure; in the night, particularly, when in bed and afar, on my terrace this music sounds as solemn, grand, and melodious.

The Naqqar Khana is also a gateway that gives access to a much larger space, originally lined by arcades, terminating in the grandest room of the palace, the Diwan-i-Am or the hall of public audience. Open on three sides, it is composed of columns and arches of red sandstone with an elevated marble throne balcony against the back wall. Inlaid in the wall behind are panels of Italian pietra dura, which were removed to the South Kensington Museum after the 1857 Rebellion but restored in 1903 on the insistence of Lord Curzon, in time for the Delhi Durbar of that year. Despite the high finish of the dressed red stone and the delicacy of the carved ornament, Bernier tells us that the columns were originally painted; and depictions of the hall dating from the late eighteenth and early nineteenth centuries seem to indicate that it was plastered and white. Bernier also tells us how the room was used:

> The Monarch every day, about noon, sits upon his throne, with some of his sons at his right and left; while eunuchs standing about the royal person flap away the flies with peacocks' tails,

agitate the air with large fans, or wait with undivided attention and profound humility to perform the different services allotted to each. Immediately under the throne is an enclosure, surrounded by silver rails, in which are assembled the whole body of Omrahs [nobility], the Rajas [regional rulers], and the Ambassadors, all standing, their eyes bent downward, and their hands crossed. At a greater distance from the throne are the Mansebdars [officials] or inferior Omrahs, also standing in the same posture of profound reverence. The remainder of the spacious room, and indeed the whole courtyard, is filled with persons of all ranks, high and low, rich and poor, because it is in this hall that the King gives audience indiscriminately to all his subjects.

This idea of the emperor's connection with the people is reinforced by the architectural geometry. A single straight line runs like a thread from the foot of the throne balcony, via the Naqqar Khana and the Chatta Chowk, to the Lahore Gate and beyond, down the principal thoroughfare of the city. It is a line of connectivity, implying the penetration of the emperor's gaze over his citizens, but also conversely suggesting his accessibility to them.

The scale and the obvious symbolism of this strict geometry raise a question about the buildings situated *beyond* the throne. Immediately behind the Diwan-i-Am lie the remains of a formal garden, facing the pavilion known as the Rang Mahal. With its carved marble basins and fountains, this large hall was the most luxurious of the palace's private apartments. It is always described as the principal building of the zenana. But can this be correct? The Rang Mahal stands on the same all-important axis, implying a function connected with the emperor personally. Mughal women are known to have been influential in court politics; but it seems unlikely that this symbolically charged spot was assigned for their use.

On the River: The Great Mughals

The interior of the Diwan-i-Am in the Red Fort, by an unknown photographer, c. 1903

Some of the earliest surviving depictions of the fort perhaps indicate an answer. Views of the palace apartments as seen from the riverside are typical of paintings made by local artists in the early nineteenth century. Often, the names of the buildings, written in Persian, are inscribed in the sky above them. But in these early works there is no 'Rang Mahal'. The building in question is clearly depicted and is labelled 'Khas Mahal', indicating that it was the private apartment of the emperor himself. The adjacent building (the one that everyone *now* calls the Khas Mahal) is labelled 'Saman Burj' (octagonal bastion).

The identification of the so-called Rang Mahal (sometimes also called the Imtiyaz Mahal) as the women's quarters is accepted by modern authorities, so it is worth investigating how and when this idea arose. The earliest expression of it that I have found occurs in an essay on the buildings of Delhi written in 1846 by the distinguished Muslim reformer, Syed Ahmad Khan. Around the same time (in 1838) the English traveller Fanny Parks was permitted to visit the room. She records that she saw 'three old women on *charpais*, looking like hags; and over the marble floor, and in the place where fountains once played, was collected a quantity of offensive black water, as if from the drains of the cook rooms'. English readers might have inferred from this passage (published in 1851) that the apartment was part of the zenana. But Parks was describing life in the palace at a time when Mughal fortunes were at their lowest ebb, with various members of the extended imperial family eking out a squalid existence. She can tell us nothing about the Mughal court in its heyday.

Of course, the paintings don't date from the heyday either. They were made 150 years after Shah Jahan's death. But they predate both Fanny Parks and Syed Ahmad Khan and show us what was believed earlier: that the finest of the palace apartments, located behind and in line with the throne, was reserved for the emperor's personal use.

The other private apartments are strung out in a line that runs from north to south, perpendicular to the axis described above, perched on the ramparts of the fort wall, overlooking the space where the river once flowed. Each is a gem in its way but outstanding in splendour is the Diwan-i-Khas, the hall of private audience. Even though it's smaller than the hall of public audience, it is no less magnificent and even richer in inlaid ornament. And though equally intended for ceremony and display, this room was also a place of work, where the emperor conferred with ministers and advisers. The nobles were required to assemble here each evening (and were fined for non-attendance) to assist the emperor as he deliberated on affairs of state. On occasion he might have preferred the greater seclusion and privacy of the Turkish baths next door. Indeed the identity of the two adjacent apartments seems to have become conflated, as Bernier calls the Diwan-i-Khas the 'gasl khana', meaning bathroom.

The arcades that enclosed a courtyard in front of the Diwan-i-Khas, below the podium, were among many parts that were lost in the wanton destruction carried out by the British after 1857. Earlier paintings may help us reconstruct parts of the palace in our minds, but the many changes carried out then make the complex hard to read. So does the slow pace of modern conservation, as the hammam, or Turkish baths, and the nearby exquisite Moti Masjid, or pearl mosque, are almost always closed. But some traces of the former atmosphere and beauty of the place are perhaps to be found in the Hayat Bakhsh Bagh, the formal garden at the northern end.

The dilapidated state of the complex is surprising in view of the iconic status that the fort holds in Indian hearts and minds. For the Lal Qila has become, at least in the eyes of the city's residents, a symbol of Delhi—perhaps even of India (after the Taj Mahal). Images of it once featured prominently on postage stamps. But its elevation to that status was not by means of the obvious process. You might fairly think that it could have achieved its iconic role on its own merits: it is an architectural masterpiece built by a great Indian imperial power in a city that has served as a capital for 800 years or more. But in today's political climate, this particular imperial power can no longer take for granted admiration for its achievements. In 2015, the name of one Mughal emperor, Aurangzeb, was unceremoniously removed from a road in central New Delhi. The Mughals alone could not make the Red Fort stand for all of India. They got help of a kind—clumsy or at best unintentional—from the British. Help came in two phases. First of all, the vandalism carried out in 1857 after the suppression of the rebellion made it—if not at the time then later, as those actions were viewed retrospectively—into a site of national resistance.

Compounding the offence ninety years later, in November 1945, the Red Fort was selected as the venue for the court martial of Shah Nawaz Khan, Prem Sahgal and Gurbaksh Singh Dhillon. These were three token individuals, selected from the many thousands of Indian officers and troops who had joined the Indian National Army and fought against the British during the Second World War. Initially fighting on the British side, they had been taken prisoner by the Japanese in Malaya, and agreed to change allegiance. Freed from jail, they joined the newly constituted INA and assisted the Japanese attack on Burma in 1945. Many members of the INA were captured by the British during that campaign. The trial of three of the officers, on charges of 'waging war against the king', provoked huge public anger, and their defence by a committee established by the Indian National Congress cemented public opinion in their support.

In the light of these events it is perhaps no wonder that the anniversary of India's Independence, achieved less than two years later, is marked annually by a speech by the prime minister standing on the ramparts of the same Red Fort. Every year on 15 August, the serving prime minister mounts Aurangzeb's barbican to address the cameras, looking down on a crowd of schoolchildren dressed in the colours of the flag, who brave the drizzle and enliven the tarmac.

On all other days of the year, a greater vibrancy and a stronger connectivity with the past are to be found in the other spectacular monument of the old city, the Jami Masjid, the vast congregational mosque commissioned by Shah Jahan. The present-day imam is a direct descendant of the mosque's first imam, appointed by the emperor over three and half centuries ago, and he asserts his authority through vocal and not always liberal interventions in social and political affairs of the day. There is rarely perfect harmony between the religious authorities and the conservation bodies who are concerned to preserve the elegant structure from the ravages of time and climate.

The Jami Masjid; photograph by Maharaja Sawai Ram Singh II, c. 1870

The elegance arises from the near-perfect proportions of the prayer hall, the covered space that appears like a detached building standing at the western end of the courtyard. Three large bulbous white domes, finely detailed with thin black vertical lines, surmount the hall where arcades of pointed arches run between the framing minarets and the central portal or iwan. Here lies the only point of tension in the composition, for the iwan is so lofty and proud that when seen from directly in front it almost obliterates the central dome. The compromise was perhaps acceptable to the architects because the function of the iwan is to broadcast the qibla, the direction of Mecca, towards the assembled faithful. This primary purpose is especially apparent on Eids or festival days, when the entire courtyard is packed with serried rows of worshippers.

At other times, the courtyard is quieter, and it offers a refuge from the bustling city that presses in on all sides. It always has done, according to Syed Ahmad Khan who describes its outer steps in the nineteenth century, thronged with market stalls, horse-traders, jugglers and storytellers. There is still a clothes market called the Meena Bazaar that obstructs part of the eastern approach. Standing apart is the grave of Maulana Azad (1888–1958), a Muslim scholar and opponent of Partition who became independent India's first minister of education. Designed by Habib Rahman, the grave is an elegant, modernist take on a traditional *chhatri*, with a sleek, minimalist white marble vaulted canopy. Nearby, in a line in front of the mosque's eastern gate, is an unsightly concrete garden, built to replace a slum settlement that was forcibly cleared during the Emergency, but which at least opens up a line of sight to connect the mosque with the Red Fort beyond, and so reminds us that it was along this route that the emperors once came to worship.

When François Bernier wrote his description of Shah Jahan's new city, its patron was still alive, but incarcerated under house arrest in the fort in Agra. An illness in the winter of 1657 prompted fears of the emperor's imminent demise and triggered a war of succession among his sons. The victor in that contest was Shah Jahan's third son Aurangzeb (r. 1658–1707). Pious and ruthless, Aurangzeb was a skilled commander and a clever strategist, who soon outmanoeuvred his brothers. Dismayed to see his father recover from his illness, he imprisoned Shah Jahan in Agra (where he died, eight years later, in 1666) and proclaimed himself the emperor in Delhi.

Throughout his long reign of half a century, Aurangzeb nursed an ambition to add the kingdoms of the Deccan to his empire and his ceaseless campaigning entailed long absences from Delhi. The city of Aurangabad became the effective capital of the empire, just as the nearby fort of Daulatabad had been in the time of Muhammad bin Tughluq, 350 years before. But on this occasion, many members of the nobility—especially the less ambitious ones—were permitted to stay back in Delhi, where they kept up a skeletal court. Delhi continued to be acknowledged as the capital. And so it was to remain through the reigns of Aurangzeb's successors.

The saddest victim of the Mughal civil war was Shah Jahan's eldest son and appointed heir, Dara Shikoh. A liberal, open-minded man, made in the mould of his great-grandfather Akbar, Dara Shikoh was a poet and a humanist. Before the war, while Aurangzeb toiled on campaign far from the court, Dara stayed by his father's side in Delhi and read Hindu scriptures such as the Vedas. On ascending the throne, Aurangzeb first humiliated his brother by parading him through Delhi's streets as a captive and then had him beheaded on a charge of heresy. But his remains were interred on the terrace of Humayun's grand tomb, and it is some small consolation to think that even in death Dara Shikoh remains a Delhiite, while Aurangzeb died and was buried in the distant Deccan.

Staying On: The Late Mughals

The eighteenth century, a time of great cultural and economic growth in various parts of India, was a depressing era for Delhi. As in the fifteenth century when Timur's sack of Delhi had weakened the centre but in doing so had given the regions a chance to flourish, so again the gradual disintegration of central authority from Delhi created a space in which new regional powers emerged. These included three so-called successor states: Lucknow in the north, Murshidabad in the east and Hyderabad in the south. In each case, a noble who was initially appointed by the centre to govern a large province of the empire, managed to assert his autonomy and establish his own dynastic succession. All three states inherited and further developed the Mughal court culture, somewhat adapted in form as the rulers of the three new dynasties happened to be Shia rather than Sunni Muslims. Hindu kingdoms old and new also grew in stature in this period. In the west, the Rajput kingdom of Jaipur reinvented itself as a modernized, economically powerful state, while the militarily successful Maratha clan of the Scindias established its domain in central India, later fixing its capital at Gwalior. This is an exciting era for enthusiasts of Indian urbanism, when fine new cities were founded in each of these regions, embellished by vast palace complexes and extensive gardens.

The Qutb Minar in an aquatint by Thomas & William Daniell published in 1808, based on drawings made by them on site in 1789.

The courtyard and screen of the Quwwatu'l-Islam mosque, painted by Robert Smith, c. 1822.

The Purana Qila from the west; aquatint by Thomas & William Daniell published in 1796, based on drawings made by them on site in 1789.

The Red Fort (Lal Qila) seen from the River Yamuna; section of a panorama by a Delhi artist, c. 1815.

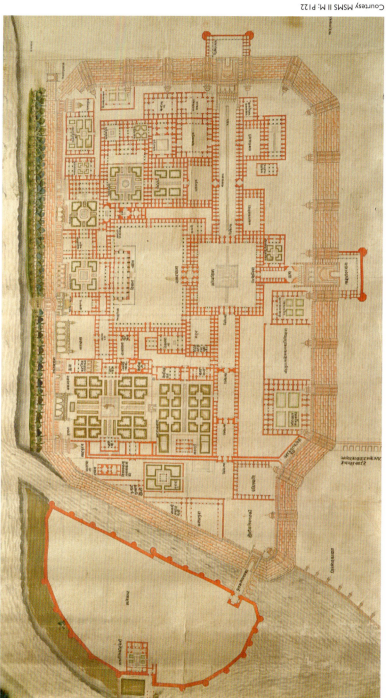

Plan of the Red Fort, drawn by a Jaipur cartographer, c. 1725.

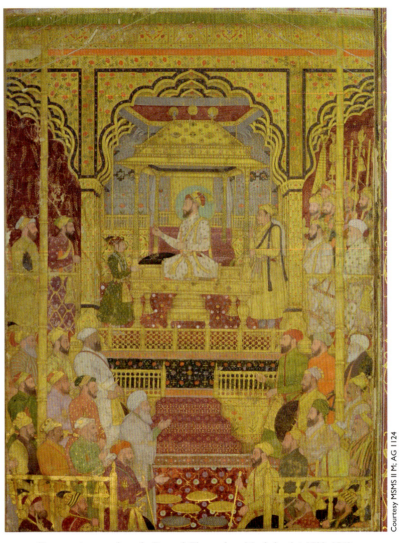
Emperor Aurangzeb on the Peacock Throne, by a Mughal artist, 1700–1750.

Jantar Mantar; aquatint by Thomas & William Daniell published in 1808, based on drawings made by them on site in 1789.

The arcades of Connaught Place, designed by Robert Tor Russell in 1931.

What a depressing contrast Delhi makes at this time! Aurangzeb was followed in rapid succession by a series of weak rulers, who were little more than puppets in the hands of their ministers. Many of them were blinded or killed by nobles or relatives. Court intrigues swung the fortunes of what remained of the empire, and throughout the century the city suffered a series of humiliations along with the court.

The death of Aurangzeb in 1707 signalled another war of succession, but on this occasion the victor, who ruled as Bahadur Shah (r. 1707–12), was already in his mid-sixties when he came to the throne and survived only a further five years. His sons in turn grappled for the throne, but the winner, Jahandar Shah, shocked everyone by marrying a dancing girl and promoting her family. He was soon dislodged and murdered by his nephew Farrukhsiyar (r. 1713–19). The replacement was no improvement: he depended heavily on certain generals and ministers who took control of the Red Fort, kept the emperor under house arrest and finally blinded and killed him. The ministers next tried out a couple of young princes of the imperial family, putting each in turn on the throne but disposing of them unceremoniously when they were deemed unfit. At last their choice fell upon a grandson of Bahadur Shah named Muhammad Shah (r. 1719–48), who lasted longer, not because he was abler or wiser but because he was entirely compliant and was content to leave the administration to incompetent advisers while he stayed in his harem.

This behaviour has done his historical reputation no harm: he is popularly known as Rangila, 'the colourful'. But the deteriorating situation in Delhi caught the attention of Nadir Shah, the man who overthrew the Safavids of Persia in 1736 and apparently thought the Mughals were ripe for the same treatment. In 1739 he invaded India, quickly overcame the token resistance of the imperial forces and occupied Delhi. He seemed more interested in loot than in staying, and Muhammad Shah still hoped to buy him off. Unfortunately, some of the city's merchants quarrelled with Nadir Shah's troops over how much they should pay for grain. Nadir Shah responded by ordering a general massacre of civilians and the burning of houses. After reducing the city to a pitiful condition, Nadir Shah packed up and left, taking with him the contents of the treasury and the gem-studded Peacock Throne, which had been made for Shah Jahan.

Muhammad Shah continued to rule for nearly a decade after Nadir Shah's departure. Prominent among the architectural embellishments added to the environs of Delhi during his reign is the observatory known as the Jantar Mantar, which was built not by the emperor but by one of the regional rulers, Maharaja Sawai Jai Singh II of Jaipur. The forms of the huge stone instruments, which the maharaja designed himself, to modern eyes suggest abstract sculpture, and their meanings to most are likely to be just as obscure. Jai Singh also built four other observatories, one in his own capital city, Jaipur, one on the roof of an ancestral property in Varanasi, and smaller ones in Mathura and Ujjain, cities where he was posted. There's one here in Delhi partly because Jai Singh had to seek the approval of the emperor to build his observatories and thereby reform the calendar and partly because this too was ancestral land. Largely undeveloped at the time—but now at the busy heart of New Delhi—the area had been acquired by his forebear and namesake Raja Jai Singh I (who served Shah Jahan and Aurangzeb) and was then known as Jaisinghpura.

Muhammad Shah was succeeded by his son Ahmad Shah (r. 1748–54) who followed suit, spending his entire time in his harem, while northern regions of the empire including Punjab and Kashmir were overrun by the Afghan commander Ahmad Shah Abdali. In his reign too, the major monument added to Delhi was built by a courtier, in this case the *vizir* or prime minister of the empire, known as Safdarjang, who established the dynasty that ruled Lucknow from the mid-eighteenth to the mid-nineteenth centuries. Prefiguring the highly ornamented architecture of that city, Safdarjang's tomb is recognizably from the same tradition as Humayun's tomb (which stands at the other end of Lodi Road), but is a playful, decorated, scaled-down rendering of the same themes. Details like the carved leaf forms that coil around the foils of the cusped arches have tempted critics to call it decadent or rococo. Such terms are unfashionable now, so let us say instead that its exuberant style is typical of its time. Significant of its time too is the fact that this, the last great Mughal mausoleum, was built not for an emperor or an empress, but for a minister who, while overseeing the disintegration of the empire he was meant to serve, carved out a kingdom and established a dynasty of his own.

In 1754 the Mughal emperor Ahmad Shah was blinded by another leading noble, Ghazi al-Din, and replaced on the throne by an elderly cousin who was given the title Alamgir II. This title was a reference to Aurangzeb, whose proper title—rarely used by modern historians—was Alamgir, or 'seizer of the universe'. Ghazi al-Din perhaps hoped to restore a semblance of order. But he was unable to manage affairs effectively through his puppet because he lacked the funds to pay the army and could not check the rising power and aggressiveness of the Marathas and the Jats, who now controlled the districts around Agra. More seriously, he could not prevent the Afghan, Ahmad Abdali from storming Delhi and looting the city. Like Nadir Shah (whom he had once served), Ahmad Abdali had not come to stay but to pick over the bones. When he left, his booty included a number of Mughal princesses. The noble Ghazi al-Din, fearing that the emperor too might fall into Ahmad Abdali's hands, coolly had him murdered. He told Alamgir II that a Sufi had taken up residence in Firuz Shah Kotla, the palace complex dating back to the time of the

Tughluqs. Ever eager to meet holy men, Alamgir II set out for the spot, only to encounter not a Sufi but an assassin. He was buried in Humayun's tomb.

His eldest son and heir, the bookish Shah Alam (r. 1759–1806), escaped both Ghazi al-Din and Ahmad Abdali by prudently fleeing from Delhi. The Marathas tried and failed to deal with the continuing threat posed by Ahmad Abdali: they suffered a crushing defeat at Panipat in 1761 (on the same field as the Mughals' original victory in 1526). Ahmad Abdali was forced to return home not by any Indian army but by his own mutinous troops. Meanwhile, Shah Alam was attempting to recover control over Bengal, as a first step in restoring the empire. Here he was halted by a new opponent: the British. In 1765, he signed the Treaty of Allahabad, which put the British in charge of the revenue of eastern India, only nominally under Mughal rule, in return for an annual pension.

Shah Alam continued to live in Allahabad until 1772, though anxious all the while to return to Delhi, not only because it was still seen as the capital but also because while fleeing he had left all his womenfolk behind in the Red Fort. They too were eager to see him return. Shah Alam's prime protectors, the British, promised and failed to help him on this score, so he turned instead to the Marathas, who were keen to recover some of their former influence.

Once he was back in Delhi, things began to improve for Shah Alam. With the support of one notably loyal noble of Persian descent, Mirza Najaf Khan, he was able to assert his authority over the empire's former heartland—from Punjab to Agra. But things fell apart after Najaf Khan died and reached a nadir in 1788. In that year, a rather less notably loyal noble of Afghan descent, one Ghulam Qadir, nursing grievances over the past treatment of his family, occupied the Red Fort. He arrested the emperor and sent his soldiers to plunder the royal apartments of the palace. Guards and servants who stood in their way were tortured or killed, and even the royal women were dragged out of the harem and abused. When the emperor complained, Ghulam Qadir blinded him, gouging out his eyes with his own hands. Other members of the imperial family, denied food and water, died of dehydration.

Rash and cruel, Ghulam Qadir was also imprudent. He had neglected to ensure an adequate supply of food even for himself and his men, and after eleven weeks of occupation he was forced to withdraw. At this point the Marathas again intervened, chasing after Ghulam Qadir and his followers. They recovered the stolen loot and returned it all to the emperor along with—an especially touching gift—Ghulam Qadir's eyeballs.

Blinding was such a common punishment because a blind man was deemed unfit to rule. In this late Mughal era, blinding became almost a routine operation. Jahandar Shah, for example, had several of his relatives blinded when he came to the throne in 1712. No doubt he thought he was being lenient: it was sufficient to blind rather than kill them because a blind man could not sit on the throne and so presented no threat. But matters had sunk so low by 1788 that the blinding of Shah Alam did not put an end to his reign. He continued as nominal emperor under the protection of the Marathas.

This situation only changed after fifteen years as a result of the long-standing rivalry for power in northern India between the Marathas and the British. In 1803, an episode in that rivalry was played out within sight of Delhi, on the east bank of the Yamuna river. An army under the command of Lord Lake forced the Marathas to withdraw from the city, and the British took over the role of protecting the emperor.

Lake found Shah Alam, 'reduced to poverty, seated under a small tattered canopy'. The emperor signed a treaty with the

British that restricted his authority to the area of the Red Fort, in return for a pension. The real administration, even of the city, lay in the hands of the British Resident, appointed as its political representative by the East India Company. Delhiites at the time must have been struck by the irony that the emperor bore the same grandiose title as the last of the Sayyid sultans, whose writ similarly had not extended beyond his own front door. The ditty about the realm of Shah Alam extending only 'from Delhi to Palam' is sometimes said to refer to this later ruler.

Shah Alam's successors, his son Akbar II (r. 1806–37) and grandson Bahadar Shah II (r. 1837–57), were styled by the British 'King of Delhi', but even that was an exaggeration. Desperate efforts were made to keep up appearances throughout these last two reigns, with the emperor and his sons parading through the city on elephants on festival days, bearing all the trappings of an imperial procession. But those who looked closely noticed that the trappings were faded and torn. The emperor's pension was simply insufficient to maintain the many members of his family in customary dignity or even normal cleanliness. Its ever-diminishing value was the subject of frequent humiliating negotiations with the British, who remained resolute in their parsimony. In a fit of frustration, the imperial prince Mirza Jahangir took a potshot at the British Resident. He was banished to Allahabad, where he drank himself to death on cherry brandy.

When Reginald Heber, bishop of Calcutta, visited the court of Akbar II, he found the great hall of audience being used as a lumber room, stacked high with broken furniture, and the throne canopy smothered in pigeon droppings. The eccentric traveller Fanny Parks was shown around parts of the palace early in the reign of Bahadur Shah and got a similar impression of the pavilion known as the Rang Mahal:

I was taken into a superb hall: formerly fountains had played there; the ceiling was painted and inlaid with gold . . . [But now] over the marble floor, and in the place where fountains once played, was collected a quantity of offensive black water, as if from the drains of the cook rooms. From a veranda, the young prince [her guide] pointed out a bastion in which the king was then asleep.

The older cities, built by the earlier sultans to the south of the Mughal walled city of Shahjahanabad, were equally by now in a state of ruin and decay. An early Assistant Resident, Charles Metcalfe, described the scene:

The ruins of grandeur that extend for miles on every side fill [the mind] with serious reflection. The palaces crumbling into dust, every one of which could tell many tales of royal virtue or tyrannical crime, of desperate ambition or depraved indolence . . . the myriads of vast mausoleums, every one of which was intended to convey to futurity the deathless fame of its cold inhabitant, and all of which are passed by unknown and unnoticed . . . these things cannot be looked at with indifference.

Such a scene was delightful to the moralizing British and to artists of picturesque landscape such as Thomas Daniell. The Daniells—Thomas and his nephew William—visited Delhi in February 1789, the year after the emperor Shah Alam was blinded, and well before the British took control of the city. The subjects that they selected to include in their subsequent series of aquatints, *Oriental Scenery* (published in 1795–1808), represent an interesting range. They include, unsurprisingly, some fine examples of Mughal architecture, such as the Jami Masjid, shown in all its imperial grandeur, along with lesser monuments such as the Chaunsath Khamba and the tombs that cluster around Humayun's. They also include more recent buildings such as the Qudsia Bagh, a garden palace to the north of Shahjahanabad built in 1748 for the emperor's mother, and two views of the Jantar Mantar. Despite their antiquarian interests—they also depicted the Qutb Minar, of course—the Daniells thus engaged with architecture of their own era. The Qudsia Bagh (today decayed almost to extinction) is shown in its pristine state (helpfully to art historians). They may not have been aware of the youth of the Jantar Mantar as they show it in a state of decay that is not credible. Similarly, they have exaggerated the decay of the Purana Qila and Firuz Shah Kotla. It is not that these forts were not in fact ruined, just that they and the surrounding terrain were not as broken as they are shown. The picturesque is an aesthetic that favours rough, irregular forms as pictorial devices, while in mood recalling Gray's elegiac warning, 'The paths of glory lead but to the grave'.

Whether the wide plain of Delhi was or was not crumbling into dust, with the dawn of the new century, the city of Shahjahanabad began to enjoy something of an economic recovery, spurred on by the more settled political conditions and the greater degree of security. The British might have been mean to the emperor, but they were not (yet) arbitrary or violent towards the citizens. Sensing that the days of sudden invasions were over, the merchants of Delhi found it worthwhile once again to invest in their businesses.

At the same time, there was a remarkable resurgence in the arts. Painters who had previously worked for the court found a new source of patronage in the British and began to produce images of Delhi's historic buildings. Among prominent exponents in Delhi of this new style, known as Company Painting, were Ghulam Ali Khan (active 1815–50) and Mazhar Ali Khan (likely a relative, active 1840–55), famous for their depictions of the Red Fort and other buildings of Delhi. The last emperor, Bahadur Shah, built a summer palace in Mehrauli (now dilapidated) and added a pavilion to the buildings of the Red Fort: a red sandstone island in the middle of the tank at the heart of the Hayat Bakhsh Bagh, which somewhat breaks the vista across the garden but is a charming reworking on a miniature scale of the idea, common in Rajput architecture, of a water palace or *jal mahal* as a place of retreat.

Even more than painting and architecture, this era is remembered for its Urdu poetry. Bahadur Shah was himself a poet who wrote under the pen name Zafar. The literary meetings (or mushairas) that he hosted in the palace attracted other luminaries, such as Mohammad Ibrahim Zauq (1788–1855) and Asadullah Khan Ghalib (1797–1869). Their poetry is suffused with a sense of loss and longing. At one level it is a collective lament for the diminished status of their world. Sometimes, Zafar addresses his own deplorable condition directly, as in his most often quoted couplet:

> I am not the apple of anyone's eye, nor the joy of any heart,
> A handful of useless dust, no purpose I discharge.

Sometimes the focus is on the city itself, and the regret is that nothing of purpose can be achieved in this place which they still cannot bear to leave. As Zauq puts it:

> Could talent live at home and thrive,
> Why should the Badakhshaan ruby wander world-wide?
> Albeit in Deccan, Zauq, the Muse commands respect,
> Who would quit the lanes of Delhi and suffer exile?

More often, though, the lament is displaced, being presented as the poet's sense of his unworthiness as a devotee of God, or his despair arising from unrequited love. In this realm, Ghalib is the master:

> A sigh needs a lifetime to make its full impact,
> Who lives long enough to conquer your ringlets?
> ... Love demands patience, desire will not wait,
> What to do with the heart till it bleeds to death!

The same theme and mood are well captured in Ahmed Ali's famous novel *Twilight in Delhi* (1940). Though written a century later, its characters are still lamenting the fall of the Mughal Empire and the decline of the city. Given the city's latitude, real twilight in Delhi is over in a matter of moments, but Delhi's metaphorical twilight is a protracted affair. The novel's protagonist Asghar falls in love with a girl on the basis of a stolen glance, and despite family opposition prevails in his determination to marry her. After his success, Asghar is disappointed to discover that his bride is a demure doe and not the seductress he had imagined from the glance. He neglects her. She falls ill, and he neglects her more. She dies. He later discovers by chance that her naughty little sister is exactly the sex kitten he craves, and that she fancies him. He begs to marry her. But her sensible parents point out that they have already given him one daughter, and he failed to take proper care of her, so he is not getting another. Misery all round!

The mournfulness that had been simmered and savoured by the poets of Bahadur Shah's court acquired a frightening new cause in 1857, when the city erupted in violence. What British writers used to call the Indian Mutiny—and Indian nationalists pointedly relabelled as the First War of

Independence—broke out in the military cantonment at Meerut, to the north of Delhi, on 10 May 1857. The revolt was to spread across large parts of northern India. Its underlying cause was the resentment against the British annexation of Indian states such as Lucknow, and both real and imagined insensitivity towards certain Indian religious and social customs. The infamous matter of the greased cartridges was a case in point. Believing the new cartridges—which had to be bitten open—to be greased with pig and cow fat, which are repugnant on religious grounds, the Indian sepoys refused to use them. In Meerut, British officers met this insubordination head-on by sentencing eighty-five sepoys to jail. To make a more effective example of them, they were humiliated by being fettered in front of their comrades. But the comrades rose in revolt, shooting the officers and releasing the prisoners. They then marched on Delhi.

The relatively small and mostly civilian British community in Delhi was taken by surprise. The rebels were able to enter the city virtually unopposed, where they stirred up a riot that led to a general massacre of Europeans. They forced their way into the Red Fort and beseeched the ageing emperor to be their leader. Bahadur Shah had his own reasons to be disaffected with the British. They had already made it clear that the charade of royalty would end with him: that after his death, his sons would retain the title of prince but none would be recognized as his successor. His domineering wife, Zinat Mahal, in her efforts to advance her own son, intrigued tirelessly against this decision and pestered her husband to reject it. Despite this, Bahadur Shah had some reservations about lending his support to the rabble now clamouring before him. But in the end he had little choice and the revolt, at least in Delhi, was conducted in his name, with the avowed aim of restoring Mughal rule.

Kashmiri Gate; photograph by Bourne & Shepherd, 1860s

The British officer in charge of the arsenal blew it up before the rebels could capture its crucial stock of arms and gunpowder. Messages were despatched to the cantonment at Ambala and to the government in Simla. In reply, an army composed of European regiments, supported by forces from the newly conquered Sikh kingdoms of the Punjab, marched on Delhi and took possession of the ridge of high ground to the north of the walled city. From this position, they orchestrated a siege.

It lasted for three months, through the hottest and then the wettest seasons of the year. Conditions within the city became intolerable. The civilian population was caught between the two sides of the conflict. No doubt many were sympathetic to the political aims of the revolt but their homes and warehouses were ruthlessly plundered by the rebels in search of supplies and cash, and they could not escape because of the siege. Both the British on the ridge and the rebels in the city were able to receive reinforcements as the weeks went by. Casualties were high in the daily skirmishes between them, and disease was ever present because of the difficulty of burying the dead. The final successful British assault on the city's northern wall began on 14 September under the command of the young Brigadier John Nicholson, who later died of his wounds. A week later the British were again in control of the whole city. Bahadur Shah was brought back under escort from Humayun's tomb where he had fled. He was later put on trial for his role in the uprising and sentenced to exile in Rangoon, where he died in 1862. Two of his sons suffered more summary justice as the arresting officer, Captain Hodson, fearing a rescue bid, shot them in the street.

Retribution by the British continued long after the recapture of the city, with hunting parties scouring the countryside in search of rebels or their sympathizers, to shoot and hang. Vengeance extended even to some of the city's buildings. A proposal to raze the Jami Masjid and replace it with a cathedral was mercifully aborted, but much wanton destruction was carried out inside the Red Fort—perceived as the focal point of the uprising—in the name of rendering it unfit for any future military use. Arcades enclosing garden courtyards were destroyed so that they could never again serve as a rebel's hiding place. Inlaid ornament in the palace pavilions was looted. The architectural historian James Fergusson raised a lonely voice of protest as 'the whole of the haram courts of the palace were swept off the face of the earth to make way for a hideous British barrack'.

These actions reveal the depth of feeling that the events of 1857 inspired. In the British public imagination, the 'Mutiny' became a tale of Indian barbarism and of British determination and pluck. The leaders that died, like Nicholson, became national heroes. Scenes of important actions, like Kashmiri Gate, where the British re-entry into the city began, were visited in a mood of reverence that is normally reserved for shrines. And this continued for generations. A guidebook by the engineer Gordon Risley Hearn, published fifty years later, describes Delhi as though the main purpose of visiting the city was to tour and reflect on the scenes of the Mutiny. Popular historians even today quote copiously from the many eyewitness records, selecting episodes that highlight individual acts of bravery in the face of Indian brutality.

The events of 1857 inspired a slew of novels. The two most famous among them—*The Siege of Krishnapur* by J.G. Farrell (1973) and *A Flight of Pigeons* by Ruskin Bond (1980)—are both modern and their action is not set in Delhi. For a more contemporary and Delhi-based perspective we must turn to a near-forgotten masterpiece of the genre, *On the Face of the Waters* by Flora Annie Steel (1896). Steel's story elaborates one of the many Mutiny myths, about an Englishman who reportedly lived in disguise within the city throughout the three months of the siege. Her manner of telling it unsettled some of her compatriots because she candidly depicts the contemptuous attitudes of many Britons in India that were among the uprising's causes. Another Mutiny myth—that Englishwomen were raped by sepoys—was widely believed long after it was officially discredited. Fear of rape became part of the British psyche in India and resurfaced in other novels including, most famously, E.M. Forster's *A Passage to India* (1929).

Feelings ran just as deep on the Indian side. Renaming the episode as the First War of Independence links it retrospectively to the heroism and sacrifice of the freedom struggle of the twentieth century. Official accounts even of the peaceful movement of Mahatma Gandhi are often prefaced by descriptions of British unfairness and cruelty back in 1857. And the monuments have been reinscribed. Literally so, in the case of the Mutiny

Memorial—a Gothic commemorative spire erected by the British on the ridge, whose original inscription speaks of the number of 'enemy' killed—where a second inscription added after Independence points out that this refers to patriotic Indians who laid down their lives. Back down on the plain, Kashmiri Gate still stands but its role in history has been overwritten as its name has been reassigned to the nearby bus terminal.

The Mutiny Memorial; photograph by Maharaja Sawai Ram Singh II, c. 1870

Starting Anew: The British

The British were late converts to the merits of Delhi as a capital. A maritime trading nation, for a long time they preferred to maintain the port city of Calcutta as their capital. For more than a hundred years after their capture of Delhi in 1803, it continued to have, in their eyes, the status of a provincial city. Before 1857 it was less important than Agra, which served as the headquarters of the North-West Provinces and was the seat of the lieutenant governor. After 1857, Delhi came under the jurisdiction of the Punjab. But slowly, and despite the trauma of 1857, the historical and geographical advantages of Delhi began to lure reluctant Britons to its cause.

The process began in 1877, when, on the suggestion of the British Prime Minister Benjamin Disraeli, Queen Victoria was declared empress of India. A grand ceremony was planned at which the new empress was represented by Viceroy Lord Lytton. Since the British were now assuming the imperial mantle, at last replacing the lately defunct Mughals, it seemed appropriate to conduct this ceremony on the Mughals' home turf—Delhi— rather than in the capital at Calcutta. The site selected was the cantonment to the north of the ridge. An 'Imperial Assemblage' of maharajas, nawabs and other representatives of the Indian people gathered together to proclaim the official inauguration of an empire that had already existed de facto for over a century.

In 1903 the operation was repeated to proclaim Edward VII as the new king-emperor. The Delhi Durbar of that year was staged by Lord Curzon on the same site and on an even grander scale. The vast tented encampment even had its own temporary railway line. Finally, in December 1911, a third Delhi Durbar was staged, and this time the new monarch, King George V, and his consort, Queen Mary, came in person to receive homage and to be crowned as emperor and empress.

In his speech on that occasion, George V announced that for 'the better administration of India and the greater prosperity and happiness of Our People' it had been decided to transfer the seat of government from Calcutta to 'the ancient Capital of Delhi'. No previous warning had been given of this announcement, and the decision had been a carefully guarded secret. The king did not elaborate on the reasons, leaving it to the people themselves to work out how it was going to make them happier and more prosperous. Some were ungrateful enough to raise doubts.

The actual if not stated reasoning went back to the disastrous partition of Bengal in 1905 by Lord Curzon, one of the last acts of

The Imperial Assemblage, Delhi; photograph by Bourne & Shepherd, 1877

his controversial viceroyalty. This was a deeply unpopular move in Bengal and led the Indian National Congress (already twenty years old) to admit the idea of constitutional change as a fit topic for discussion. It marked, in short, the coming of age of Indian political nationalism. The British had resolved to reverse the partition, but the reunification was to be coupled with the transfer of the capital so as to save face, to give the king something new and positive rather than apologetic to announce in his speech.

Some commentators touted the supposed climatic advantages of Delhi over Calcutta. The insufferable Bengal summer caused the entire administration to decamp to Simla for more than half the year. But the transfer to Delhi did not lift the need for this annual migration. As the climate was marginally better, the period in Simla could be reduced from seven months to five; and the journey was shorter. But it was really the political climate of Bengal that the British sought to escape by the move to Delhi. They hoped that compliant Delhiites would provide a more

The 1911 Delhi Durbar: the procession passes the Jami Masjid; unknown photographer, 1911

congenial atmosphere than truculent Bengalis in which to carry on the work of the empire.

That Delhi's historical associations were also found attractive is revealed by the king's description of it as 'the ancient capital'. The move in large part was about reshaping the empire, presenting it with a fresh face that would appear more Indian. The domed pavilions and other trappings of the three Delhi Durbars had all been constructed in a quasi-Mughal style. King George and Queen Mary sat on thrones on the ramparts of the Red Fort to present themselves to the watching crowds, and were attended by young Indian princes serving as pages. The decision to inhabit and rebuild Delhi as the capital carried forward the process of refashioning the British Empire in India in a local style. There are not many moments in history when the British took major

King George V and Queen Mary on the ramparts of the Red Fort with Indian princes as pages; postcard issued by J. Beagles & Co., in commemoration of the 1911 Delhi Durbar

decisions with such a large aesthetic component. But by the early twentieth century, against a rising tide of Indian nationalism, Palladian Calcutta looked just too foreign, and its location spoke too loudly of trade, of the commercial and opportunistic origins of British rule. To rule as emperors required a recognized emperor's seat, and this Delhi provided.

If the move was intended as some sort of gesture of appeasement to Indian sentiment, then the political symbolism was evidently lost on at least some residents of Delhi. A year after the king's speech, Lord Hardinge, the viceroy, made a triumphal entry into the city on the back of an enormous elephant. As he turned the corner into Chandni Chowk—the main thoroughfare of the walled city—someone threw a bomb at him. Hardinge was badly injured. His wife, sitting next to him, was miraculously unscathed. But the poor Indian mace bearer, standing behind them, was blown to pieces.

Undeterred, Hardinge persisted in his vision of a truly Indian capital, demanding that the principal buildings themselves should be designed in an Indian style. The idea did not come out of nowhere. In various Indian cities since the 1870s, British architects and engineers had been experimenting with revivals of India's historical styles of architecture, creating a new hybrid that was often dubbed 'Indo-Saracenic'. Hardinge, along with many other prominent political figures including the king, thought that adopting an Indo-Saracenic approach in the new capital would convey the essentially Indian character of the British Raj to the Indian public.

Edwin Lutyens, the architect appointed to design the new Viceroy's House, was appalled at the suggestion. In a letter to his wife, he wrote, in apparent exasperation, 'God did not make the Eastern rainbow pointed, to show his wide sympathies!' What this implies is that for Lutyens the form of the Western classical arch, like that of the rainbow, was natural if not ordained, and you couldn't mess around with it just to show how nice and accommodating you are. He doesn't spell out exactly what prompted this outburst but one can well imagine Hardinge taking him aside and saying something along the lines of, 'My dear fellow, I well understand that you are committed to round arches and that they are frightfully classical and all, but you may have noticed that around here they tend to have pointy tops, and there are some people—and I have to tell you His Majesty agrees with them—who think we ought to do them like that too, so that the Indians don't see us as alien.' However he actually expressed it, there is a remarkable historical resonance here. Seven hundred years earlier, Qutb-ud-din Aibak had taken his Indian masons aside and explained that he wanted a screen of pointed arches along the western side of his mosque. His intention was to make the building look less Indian, more foreign. And now, seven hundred years later, another prelate was giving the same instruction for the opposite purpose. The meaning of a symbol can change. The pointed arch was now proposed as a means to proclaim the alien ruler's Indian identity.

In the event, Lutyens managed to avoid the pointed arch, though not all Indian forms. And there were other things that Hardinge said that equally dismayed him. Impatient to know whether the works could be completed within his own term in office, Hardinge asked him what the buildings would look like in three years' time. Reporting this in another private letter home, Lutyens protested, '300 is what I think of . . . This is building an Imperial City!' For him, the project was on a par with the Roman Forum. And it followed that the Western classical style was the only fitting way of building it. He felt Indian architecture offered him no suitable models for imitation, and he dismissed it all as 'veneered joinery'. What was required, he insisted, was 'logic, and not the mad riot of the tom-tom'.

His partner on the project, Herbert Baker, had worked for many years on the government buildings in Pretoria and was similarly a committed classicist, who was sceptical of the usefulness of 'the primitive and charming methods' of Indian architecture. But their scruples were overwhelmed by the most extraordinary public debate. It wasn't just the viceroy making a suggestion. Politicians in both Britain and India, architects, arts experts, connoisseurs and leader-writers argued the merits of the various possible approaches. On one side of the argument, some claimed that the British should tread in the footsteps of Alexander the Great and take European civilization to Asia. Others retorted that their first commitment should be to India and its own traditions. Passionate speeches were delivered in Parliament. Public meetings were held to discuss the virtues of Indian craftsmanship. Petitions signed by eminent authors were published in the press. At no other point in history have the English people been so obsessed with matters of architecture. Lutyens's frequent caustic comments on all this unlooked-for advice—'no one in India knows any kind of craftsmanship except accountancy'—merely fanned the flames.

On the sidelines of this debate, two dissenting arguments went almost unheard. The first, led by Lord Curzon, insisted that transferring the capital was a terrible idea in the first place and should be scrapped. Curzon correctly predicted that it would take far longer and cost far more than planned. He also perhaps saw that the Victoria Memorial Hall in Calcutta, which he himself had commissioned, to serve not just as a monument to the late empress but as a symbol of the empire, would soon be overshadowed and rendered provincial. The second argument, promoted by the arts educator and polemicist E.B. Havell, was that the buildings of New Delhi should not just be in an Indian style; they should be designed by Indian architects. If the idea is to give the place an

Indian character, he said, let the Indians make it themselves. In the face of the official government riposte to this proposal—that no Indian architect was competent to carry out the work—a flurry of research was undertaken to demonstrate the viability of the idea, but no one in government ever took it seriously.

So it came down to an argument, not about agency but about style. And if a debate about architectural style seems not to be a typically British thing, the outcome was more obviously so: it was a compromise. The Viceroy's House and the All-India War Memorial (or India Gate) designed by Lutyens, and the twin Secretariats and the Council House (or Parliament building) designed by Baker adhere to the Western classical tradition, but with certain Indian elements worked in. Chief among these is the material, the buff and red sandstone quarried in Dholpur, that echoes the similar stone used in the city's great sultanate and Mughal monuments such as Humayun's tomb and the Qutb Minar. Both Lutyens and Baker adopted the typical Indian chajja—a stone blade that juts out at the eve to protect the façade from sun and rain. And the rooflines of their buildings are dotted with chhatris, or domed kiosks. 'Chattris are stupid, useless things,' Lutyens protested; but he used them. The capitals of his columns at Viceroy's House are fluted and bell-shaped like some very early Indian examples, while the outline of the great dome and the mouldings on its drum are modelled on the tumulus and railings of the Buddhist stupa at Sanchi.

The two architects described their compromise in rather different ways. Baker's declared aim was 'to weave into the fabric of the more elemental and universal [by which he meant Western] forms of architecture the threads of such Indian traditional shapes and features as are compatible with the nature and use of the building'. One might detect some half-heartedness in the idea of 'compatible shapes'. And his notion of 'Indian traditional features' seems to include a large quantity of elephant heads, which no doubt qualify in a literal sense but evoke Indian pageantry more than architecture, and which he does not so much 'weave into the fabric' as plaster over the surface. The two Secretariat buildings—North and South Blocks—face each other across the central axial way, their façades enriched by deep elevated porticos that surge forward in a great Baroque gesture that would have startled even Christopher Wren. And just in case you don't get the fundamental Englishness and imperiousness of it all, the inscription around the entrance portal of North Block reads, 'Liberty will not descend to a people. A people must raise themselves to Liberty. It is a right that must be earned before it can be enjoyed.' So don't be in too much of a hurry then, eh? And meanwhile, to make you feel at home, here's another elephant head.

Lutyens formulated his goal more abstractly: 'to express modern India in stone, to represent her amazing sense of the supernatural, with its complement of profound fatalism.' This doesn't sound like him. It sounds more like something scripted for him by his wife, Lady Emily Bulwer-Lytton (daughter of the former viceroy, Lord Lytton), who was a theosophist. Lutyens's engagement with Indian spiritualism might best be summarized by his description of a visit from his wife's friend Annie Besant as like having 'Sunday every day of the week'. But—for all his protests and his loudly expressed contempt—he did engage with Indian architecture. He looked at selected forms with an artist's eye, not to copy them but to streamline and transform them into something new. The single word of his mission statement that rings true is 'modern'. There is no doubting that Viceroy's House is a twentieth-century building.

Critics at the time and since, comparing the contributions of Lutyens and Baker, have generally credited Lutyens with the

Viceroy's House, designed by Edwin Lutyens, has become Rashtrapati Bhavan; photograph by the author, 1986

Secretariat, North Block, designed by Herbert Baker; photograph by the author, 1986

loftier aim and the finer achievement. The contemporary writer Robert Byron thought that Baker's handling of Indian details was superficial, that it amounted to 'writing in symbols'; and he mocked his use of stone screens or jalis, which reminded him of fishnet stockings. The Council House (or Parliament House) is simpler in design and less ornamented than the Secretariats. Its circular form aims again at classical grandeur but is unfortunately inclined to suggest the motion of a spinning top instead. Evenly spaced columns in a ring unavoidably suggest motion, as Christopher Wren realized two and a half centuries earlier while designing the dome of St Paul's. The solution—adopted by Wren—is to insert periodic infills, to act as brake pads. Baker must have known this but chose not to follow Wren's example.

At the far end of Rajpath (formerly called Kingsway) stands the All-India War Memorial, now generally called India Gate. Designed by Lutyens in 1921, it commemorates 60,000 Indian soldiers who gave their lives overseas during World War I. It is inscribed with the names of the 13,516 'missing': those, whether British or Indian officers and men, who died on the North-West Frontier and in the Third Afghan War of 1919 and whose bodies were never found. As in other memorials of that time, especially those designed by Lutyens, the names are listed without distinction of race or creed. The building bears no religious symbols. Modelled on the triumphal arches of Rome (and later European derivatives like the Arc de Triomphe in Paris), it was meant to appear, above all, imperial.

Under its arch lies the single symbolic grave of an unknown soldier, with a perpetual flame. The small dome over the top of the arch (barely visible from the ground) was intended, in the original design, to emit a continuous plume of smoke, turning the monument into a gigantic incense stick.

Behind the gate stands a tall, slender pavilion or canopy, designed—again by Lutyens in 1936—to house a memorial statue of King George V. The statue was removed after Independence, and since then the canopy has remained empty because the most obvious candidate to replace the king is the 'Father of the Nation', Mahatma Gandhi, for whom such a grandiose setting is generally deemed incongruous.

In recent times, India Gate has acquired a new role as a place of peaceful public protest, a shrine of the people's conscience, like the Lincoln Memorial in Washington or London's Trafalgar Square. Sometimes the cause is very focused and personal. When a young model was murdered by a politician's son in 1999, and the investigating agencies and the courts seemed hamstrung, people gathered here in large crowds to demand that the case not be buried with the girl, that they be told who killed her. As a result of this public pressure, a conviction duly followed. Whether it is India Gate's solemn dignity or merely the ample open surrounding space that made people select it as their site of protest is hard to say. What is clear is that this fine invented tradition has given the already iconic arch a new meaning. *Rang de Basanti*, a Hindi movie that was released in 2006, the same year that the model's murderer was eventually convicted, and whose story concerns the personal and political conscience of young people in Delhi, includes a scene where the principal characters drive around India Gate in a mood that is at once earnest and joyful.

The central vista that runs from the Viceroy's House and the Secretariats to India Gate forms the core axis of New Delhi. Almost as controversial as the style of these main buildings was the development of the city's layout or plan. First came the matter of the site. It was initially assumed that the nucleus of the city would be the Civil Lines, the area beyond the old walled city, by the ridge. This had been the main area of English settlement since the early nineteenth century (though it had even earlier been a place of Mughal gardens). This was where the king–emperor laid the symbolic foundation stone after his speech at the Durbar, and this was the temporary base where Hardinge moved his government during the period of construction. Its association with the events of 1857 also invested it with much emotional significance for the British.

But the planning committee, which included Lutyens, thought that these were all good reasons to abandon it. It was too constricted, too bound up with the past. After considering various options, they selected a site to the south, an open plain, not too cluttered with existing structures and overlooked from the west by a low hill called Raisina. Standing on its crest, looking east towards the river, Lutyens saw enough space to realize the kind of plan he had in mind.

It is a great geometrical extravaganza, with long, straight ceremonial vistas, one vast sweeping curve at the back, and roads emanating at angles from roundabouts to meet the corners of interlocking hexagons. It is a pattern, designed to appeal on the page, rather than a response to topography or to considerations of need. Some historic monuments, such as the Purana Qila, are locked into the pattern and given a supporting role, like attendant follies, and Raisina and the river frame it, but it makes little other reference to the landscape. A number of different ideas inform its design. Most obviously, the scale, the grandeur and the geometry follow a Beaux Arts tradition of city planning. But the lack of density in terms of buildings—the main ceremonial route is flanked by lawns rather than buildings, for example— derives more from the English tradition of garden cities. And the bungalows on huge plots, each surrounded by a boundary wall (and often a guard), are reminiscent of the cantonments of British India.

This area is still commonly called the Lutyens Bungalow Zone (or LBZ)—a slight misnomer as the bungalows were designed by assistants, though the overall plan was his. Its lack of density remains a matter of controversy. Some insist that its green and open character is under threat as individual plots are gradually being redeveloped. But others feel that such openness is anyway inappropriate for the capital of such an enormous country, and happily contemplate the bungalows all being swept away (perhaps along with the politicians and bureaucrats who are privileged to live in them) and replaced by tightly packed high-rises. Perhaps they just mean to provoke, but they are right in regarding Delhi as a city with an empty core. As you move out from the peaceful centre, the housing colonies and suburbs become increasingly dense and teeming.

Arguments about conservation and development in New Delhi invariably invoke the name of Lutyens, as if its preservation is something owed to him as the presiding genius. There are some people who insist that such reverence is unwarranted, that greater credit should be given not just to the many other architects who designed the buildings of New Delhi, but to the viceroys and officials who oversaw their construction, and to the Punjabi contractors who actually put them together. Quite right. But it is also worth pointing out that if Lutyens has consistently enjoyed a high reputation in Delhi, the same is not true in his own country. Architectural opinion in post-war Britain was dominated by people like Sir Nikolaus Pevsner and Sir John Summerson, men of discernment but whose sympathies lay with the International Modern Movement, and for whom Lutyens's historicism (to say nothing of his politics) made him anathema. When they wrote the history of British architecture, they simply ignored him as an anachronism, an irrelevance. The American architect and theorist Robert Venturi acknowledged the genius of Lutyens as early as the 1960s, but it was another twenty years before writers like Gavin Stamp brought his work back into the view of the general public in Britain.

Lutyens's fall from grace among British intellectuals would have astonished his colleague, Herbert Baker. Reflecting on the place of New Delhi in the broad sweep of Indian history, Baker declared, 'In 2000 years there must be an Imperial Lutyens tradition in Indian architecture.' The remark shows untypical generosity towards his colleague and sometime rival, acknowledging the younger architect's superior powers of design. Allowing for some exaggeration, the idea might have seemed plausible at the time, in view of some of the city's recent buildings. Because, working alongside Lutyens and Baker were numerous assistants who at various times set up independent practices and won commissions to design major new buildings, many of which reflect in some measure the influence of the Lutyens style.

They include the Cathedral of the Redemption, designed by Henry Medd in 1928, whose interlocking geometrical volumes are clearly inspired by Lutyens's treatment of massing. The success of the design rests on its lack of fuss. There is just so much embellishment as is required to articulate an entrance—no more—and no fear of plain surfaces. In this it resembles the modern classical aesthetic of Lutyens, achieved, for example, in his design of Hyderabad House, a palace for the Nizam of Hyderabad. St Martin's Garrison Church, designed by A.G. Shoosmith in 1928–30, takes the process a step further, creating a remarkable abstracted form. When Shoosmith told Lutyens that he proposed to use only brick, Lutyens's advice was to 'Go for the Roman wall'. He meant avoid the decorative Queen Anne Revival ornament that was then so much in fashion in Britain. The detailing, where it exists, is sternly architectural, a reworking of the lines of classical mouldings, as Lutyens himself had done with consummate virtuosity at India Gate.

The Cathedral Church of the Redemption, designed by Henry Medd in 1928; photograph by the author, 1991

Perspective of Jaipur House, New Delhi, designed by C.G. and F.B. Blomfield; from the *Journal of the Indian Institute of Architects*, April 1938

Closest to the style of the master is Jaipur House, designed by C.G. Blomfield, assisted by his brother Francis, for the Maharaja of Jaipur in 1936. It is so close indeed that it has often been wrongly attributed to Lutyens himself (or assumed to be by him). But the *Journal of the Indian Institute of Architects*, when reporting its completion in 1938, clearly attributed it to the Blomfields; and one of the original signed blueprints survives in the archives of the City Palace in Jaipur. The blocky massing of the main building, especially around the dome, is very reminiscent of Lutyens, while the materials and colour scheme also signal a clear attempt to harmonize with the buildings of both Lutyens and Baker. The decorative screen that surrounded the (now sadly destroyed) swimming pool in the garden was a free copy of a screen in the Mughal Gardens behind Viceroy's House.

Lutyens-style massing was carried forward by Walter George in buildings such as the Modern School (1936), where the deep shade created by the overhanging chajja pays homage to the similar lighting effects in Viceroy's House. Lutyens, with a touch of Shoosmith, emerges again in St Stephen's College, designed by George in 1938. It is like a mini St Martin's.

So there *was* a Delhi Lutyens school, but not the general and lasting tradition imagined by Baker. There could not be because these works were outnumbered by those of the Delhi Public Works Department under Robert Tor Russell who adopted a more traditional and prosaic neoclassical style in conspicuous buildings such as the Eastern and Western Courts (1922); the official residence of the commander-in-chief (1930; later used by Jawaharlal Nehru, and now a library and museum known as Teen Murti Bhavan); and the main commercial centre, Connaught Circus (1931).

The irony is that while the rapid construction of all these buildings—government offices, courts, churches, shops and homes—looks like assembling the infrastructure of an empire that was meant to last, they actually provided one of the scenes for its political dismantling. The last thirty years of British rule saw frantic building in New Delhi alongside a process of negotiation and protest that led inevitably to departure; and both were played out against the backdrop, of course, of two world wars.

It is a difficult period to summarize. But if viewed from a Delhi perspective, certain moments appear salient. By 1917, when construction (delayed by World War I) was still in its early stages, the British government under Lloyd George was already committed to the principle of Indian self-rule within the empire. The Montagu–Chelmsford Reforms of 1919 increased the authority of provincial councils and established a Central Legislative Assembly. This decisive step towards sharing power with elected representatives created the need for the Council House designed by Baker, and explains its curious position, off axis from the other main buildings: it was an afterthought, added after the main plan had been drawn up. Originally designed to house both the new assembly and the Chamber of Princes, it is now called Sansad Bhavan and houses both the Rajya Sabha and the Lok Sabha, the two houses of India's Parliament.

The 1920s, the period when the Viceroy's House and the government buildings were being erected, was marked by protest across India, from the civil disobedience campaign of 1920 to Mahatma Gandhi's Salt March of 1930. When New Delhi was ceremonially inaugurated by Viceroy Lord Irwin on 13 February 1931, delegates were still returning to India from the first of the three Round Table Conferences held in London (1930–32), which charted India's route to dominion status. Despite the further twists along the way, and the major diversion caused by World War II, the path was then set that led eventually to the appointment of Lord Mountbatten as the last viceroy and to the achievement of India's independence in 1947.

On the night of 14 August, shortly before the midnight moment of freedom, independent India's first prime minister, Jawaharlal Nehru delivered his famous 'tryst with destiny' speech to the constituent assembly sitting in Baker's building. Outside, joyous crowds thronged the ceremonial way planned by Lutyens. What might have been the symbols of a great empire were transformed at the stroke of the midnight hour into the foundation stones of a new nation.

Partition and Growth: Independent India

Delhi changed from being an imperial city to the capital of a free nation overnight. Sadly, not all aspects of the transition were so smooth. The price of Independence was the partition of Bengal in the east and of Punjab in the west, to create the two separate parts of Pakistan. The plan was drawn up and the lines determined on the basis of the religious identity of the existing population. The idea was to include regions that were predominantly Muslim in the two parts of Pakistan. So, a point that is often forgotten, initially large-scale migrations were not expected. The solution offered to those who found themselves on the wrong side of the line was a promise to safeguard the rights of religious minorities within each of the new states.

But the people themselves were understandably mistrustful. If the division was to be on religious lines, many wanted to be with their own kind. They packed and started to move, in what became one of the largest migrations in human history. Estimates vary but at least twelve million people—and possibly twice that number—crossed the two borders. As they had to abandon their land, their homes and their employment, gathering only the few chattels they could carry to head off into the unknown, passions ran high.

Reports and rumours of confrontations sparked revenge attacks. There were violent clashes between passing columns of refugees and terrible massacres on trains and in the streets of previously peaceful neighbourhoods. Again the figures are disputed, but at least half a million—possibly many more—men, women and children were slaughtered.

The impact of this on Delhi was immense. Punjab was on Delhi's threshold (indeed Delhi was once administratively a part of Punjab). Many of those migrating from cities like Lahore and Multan, now in Pakistan, made straight for the capital, in search of a new life to replace what they had been forced to leave behind. The population of Delhi, which was less than half a million at the start of the century (before the transfer of the capital) had crept up to a million by 1947. With Partition the population doubled to two million almost overnight. The new arrivals crowded first into the refugee camps in the Purana Qila and Kingsway Camp (north of the old city, near the present Delhi University campus) and then settled in the new colonies built specially for them by the government, such as Lajpat Nagar, Rajinder Nagar and the aptly named Punjabi Bagh. As they established themselves and began to flourish, these immigrants changed the balance of the city's identity. The old culture of the established Muslim families of Shajahanabad was eclipsed by a new culture which struck many by comparison as rootless and displaced, and perhaps a touch provincial.

The effects of the influx are still with us. The population of the National Capital Region in 2017, seventy years after Partition, was approaching twenty million, ten times what is was then. But still, at the time of writing, everyone has a friend or a neighbour or a relative who came from Punjab back in 1947 with nothing. Sometimes they speak longingly of their fathers' orchards and of the fine mansions they grew up in, and a little ruefully of the hard life they had to endure on reaching Delhi. To be sure, there was optimism in the air in Delhi in the 1950s, when Nehru ruled, but the hope was about long-term investment in the future not about immediate gains, and for many the lifestyle was somewhat austere.

With the passing of the generations the Punjabi identity has not been diluted. The immigrants' grandchildren, who now flock the halls of Delhi's colleges in jeans and T-shirts, proudly identify themselves as Delhiites. They may know nothing of their grandparents' birthplaces, but they bear Punjabi names and eat Punjabi food, and on formal family occasions don Punjabi clothes and perform the same rituals as their forefathers. Theirs is a culture in permanent exile that has taken over its assumed home.

When Nehru addressed the nation at Independence, he urged his compatriots to commit themselves to 'the service of India'. Though conscious of the 'trackless centuries' of India's past, he saw his own time as a moment 'when we step out from the old to the new'. But he warned that the 'future is not one of ease or resting but of incessant striving': 'we have to labour and to work ... to build the noble mansion of free India'.

Many believed him, and perhaps more readily in Delhi, a city that was ancient but also new and quite visibly still under construction. Despite the burden of history, so much seemed to be missing to those looking out on an unfinished urban landscape. So they joined hands to build the political, cultural and financial institutions of the future. Under the guidance of B.R. Ambedkar, they framed a new constitution that turned India into a republic in 1950 and founded the universities, the museums, the handicraft boards and academies of music, dance and drama that Delhi had never had.

The spirit of optimism persisted, to some extent, during the early administrations of Nehru's daughter and eventual successor as prime minister, Indira Gandhi, in the late 1960s and early 1970s.

Threats loomed in the international arena, with the Indo-China border dispute of 1962 and the Indo-Pakistan war of 1965. But even that outlook seemed less worrisome by 1971, when renewed conflict with Pakistan led to the emergence of its eastern portion as the independent state of Bangladesh, with Indian support, despite the doubts of American and other international opinion about India's motives. Indira Gandhi's resolute stand earned her immense popularity at home.

But within a few years, her increasingly autocratic style of governance, political cronyism and the lack of economic development created a spiral of disillusionment. The nadir was reached in June 1975 when Mrs Gandhi declared a state of emergency, to pre-empt court action against her and to enable her to rule by diktat. It lasted nearly two years until March 1977, during which period many of her political opponents and vocal critics including journalists spent time cooling their heels in Tihar Jail. Important policy decisions were made arbitrarily by unelected people she appointed, including her younger son, Sanjay. Concerned about demographers' doomsday predictions about the likely effect of India's population growth, Sanjay organized a ruthless sterilization campaign. As productive householders were unwilling to come forward, his officials targeted the vulnerable—the elderly and children—to meet their target quotas. There were many other such abuses. It all ended with Mrs Gandhi's removal from power—indeed the ejection of the Congress party from office for the first time since Independence—and her own eventual incarceration in Tihar.

Mrs Gandhi recovered from the Emergency and served again as the prime minister in the early 1980s. But Delhi—the hothouse of Indian politics—never fully recovered from the trauma of those days. Today, there are leaders of national parties whose careers were forged in the crucible of student protest during the

Emergency and for whom the first (and sometimes it seems the only) principle of political morality is opposition to the Congress, whoever the Congress today happens to be or what it stands for. There are elderly journalists and commentators who still exude nothing but bile towards anyone or any institution associated with Mrs Gandhi (though one or two who still maintain that she and young Sanjay were just doing their best). And much of the population of Delhi is resigned to cynicism about politicians, convinced that their only purpose is to seize and hold on to power for their own sake, at the cost of the common good.

Their fears seem well founded when the politics turns violent and the politicians look away. Mrs Gandhi's ill-judged decision in 1984 to storm the Golden Temple in Amritsar—then occupied by Sikh separatists—led to her assassination in the grounds of her residence at the hands of her Sikh bodyguards. This act in turn provoked anti-Sikh riots in the streets and suburbs of Delhi, which leading politicians, if they did not actually orchestrate, took insufficient action to prevent. Mrs Gandhi's replacement as prime minister by her elder son Rajiv—an airline pilot by chosen profession and a political innocent with boyish good looks—briefly ignited a flicker of hope, as his approach to governance was technocratic and apparently without guile. But that hope was extinguished when Rajiv Gandhi was in turn assassinated by Sri Lankan Tamil separatists while campaigning in Tamil Nadu in 1991.

Strangely, despite the dismal outlook politically and economically, the 1980s and early 1990s were a time of cultural revival in Delhi, with new ideas in fashion and design and new approaches to heritage. The changing architecture of the city provides the largest, and most solid and enduring sign of all this. To explain the emergence of the new mood we must first backtrack a little.

In the decade after Independence, Delhi's architects seemed content to look back to Lutyens for inspiration, as in the Supreme Court which was designed by G.B. Deolalikar in 1955. And there were some other touches of historicism, as in E.B. Doctor's Ashoka Hotel of 1956, where Mughal-style ornamental stonework seems to evoke the manner of the Indo-Saracenic movement of fifty years before. Sacred architecture in the city kept to its own track, updated in terms of materials but rigidly archaic in its imagery, as in the Lakshminarayan (or 'Birla') temple of 1956.

And then came Le Corbusier's Chandigarh and everything changed. To be fair, the impact of Chandigarh is sometimes overstated. The International Modern Movement had made some earlier forays into India—most notably in Bombay—for example, in the work of Claude Batley (slightly surprisingly in view of his more historical approach in his teaching). There is also the justly famous Golconde by Antonin Raymond in Pondicherry (1936) and some other scattered examples, such as the Manik Bagh in Indore by Eckart Muthesius (1933). But the building of Chandigarh in the 1950s marked a change because of its scale. The practice on Indian soil of Le Corbusier, the modern movement's leading and most charismatic exponent, had a profound impact on a generation of Indian architects: it made them look at architecture in new ways. In Delhi, one might cite as examples that are particularly close to the master's aesthetic some works by Shiv Nath Prasad, such as Akbar Hotel (1965) in Chanakyapuri, the Shri Ram Arts Centre (1966) at Mandi House, and Tibet House (1974) on Lodi Road. Among other successful examples, one might cite the Intercontinental (now Oberoi) hotel by Durga Bajpai and Piloo Mody (1958) and the New Delhi Municipal Council (the old Civic Centre) by Kuldip Singh (1965); and the

Akbar Hotel in Chanakyapuri, designed by Shiv Nath Prasad in 1965; photograph by the author, 1987

(less successful) Inter State Bus Terminus by Rajinder Kumar (1969) and Nehru Place by Ratan Singh (as late as 1980).

Le Corbusier was not alone. The work of the American architect Louis Kahn in Ahmedabad had a comparable impact. The extension to Modern School by Jasbir and Rosemary Sachdev (1975) has been hailed as a skilful reworking of Walter George's original idiom, but one could be forgiven for mistaking a view of the building for a picture of Kahn's Indian Institute of Management in Ahmedabad (1962–70), with its scooped-out circles and exposed brickwork.

Brick is an old and respectable material. It is not in itself modernist. But in the Indian context brick had not hitherto been seen as elite. When used in great public buildings in the past, brick was usually concealed behind a facing of another material such as dressed stone. Louis Kahn showed how it could be used for prestigious buildings. Architects in Delhi took his cue, applying it in all sorts of educational and institutional buildings as well as private homes. Among the best known examples are the student hostels at Jawaharlal Nehru University by C.P. Kukreja (1970–76) and the Belgian Embassy by Satish Gujral (1983).

By the early 1980s, some architects were beginning to question the hitherto unquestioned imitation of the masters of the International Modern Movement. They woke up to the point that their imitation of major works by Le Corbusier and Louis Kahn was largely a matter of appearances—of copying or adapting their manner—rather than fully assimilating the logic and philosophy of modern design. To be sure, some had adopted the excruciating rhetoric of modernism in their writings too, but in their designs the adherence to modernism was sometimes forced or superficial. The previously proclaimed universal applicability of modernism was being questioned even in the West, which had nurtured it. How much more urgent it now seemed to challenge this in a country like India which had a different developmental path.

The question that became so pressing in the 1980s and early 1990s was how to move Indian architecture ahead, keeping a hold on the technological and other material benefits of the International Modern Movement, while at the same time trying to restore something of the broken thread of a distinctively Indian tradition. Restoring the thread was not about archaism or atavism. The new quest was not a leap backwards into the past. It was about trying to find a way to be both recognizably Indian and modern at once.

But who were the exemplars who could show the way down that difficult track? Was there anyone after Independence who had accomplished—or even attempted—such a task before? Well,

Partition and Growth: Independent India

The India International Centre, designed by Joseph Allen Stein in 1959; photograph by the author, 1991

in Delhi there was Joseph Allen Stein, an architect of Californian origin, who had long been settled in India, quietly pursuing his own distinctive and highly individual approach. His prominent successes in the city include the arts centre known as Triveni Kala Sangam (1957), the India International Centre (1959) and the Ford Foundation (1966). The use of stone, of coloured tiles, and of cooling devices such as the jali, and the integration of gardens and buildings all point to his sensitive reading and reinterpretation of aspects of the Indian tradition. But these buildings are far from historical pastiche: their visual idiom is also modern. His some-time partner on these projects, Habib Rahman, produced comparable works independently, such as Rabindra Bhavan (1959).

Highly regarded—as well as personally liked—within the profession, Stein and Rahman showed a way, and soon every architect and critic was talking about the Indian identity and the historical thread. Eminent historians like Romila Thapar were sought out and asked to give their endorsements, certificates on the authenticity of the traditional qualities of contemporary designs. Heady days, indeed.

One of the most articulate voices on this topic was that of Charles Correa. Although his practice was based in Bombay (now Mumbai), he left his mark on Delhi, and deserves mention here. Correa's engagement with Delhi is, in truth, a bit of a puzzling mixture. He was responsible for the planning of the Crafts Museum at Pragati Maidan (1975), a project that put him in touch with India's unblemished rural traditions.

However, it did not appear to have had much impact on him when he designed the Life Insurance Corporation building in Connaught Place (built in the mid-1980s). With its cascades of mirror glass and suspended space frame, it apes the fashionable gimmicks of contemporary architecture in the West. It was greeted with dismay by students of Delhi's architecture schools who felt let down by this maestro who spoke so eloquently of India's proud traditions. Correa helped orchestrate exhibitions like *Vistara* (1986) which presented Indian architecture as a seamless and distinctive whole; in which images of stepwells and wall tiles and row houses were juxtaposed with drawings of mandalas and mazes, irrespective of date and place, to present a seemingly cohesive, timeless and potent whoosh of Indian identity. Young architects were terribly excited by the potential of it all. So when the LIC building went up, they gazed in horror and demanded, 'Where's the whoosh?' The eminent critic Hasan-Uddin Khan tried to redeem it by describing the building's two main blocks as forming a giant 'darwaza' or gateway linking Connaught Place to the rest of Delhi. Nobody believed him—least of all the armed guard who prevents members of the public from using the building as a route. Hasan-Uddin's comment, written in 1987, is chiefly significant as an indication of how desperate everyone had become to find a historical antecedent for each and every design.

Correa fared much better with his building for the British Council (1992). No doubt the cutaway façade still retains a Le Corbusian feel, if softened by the mural of a banyan tree by the British artist Howard Hodgkin. But the courtyard at the rear is a more satisfying reworking of Indian spaces and motifs, with a particularly pleasing play of light. The warm red sandstone cladding—despite the baldness of the unmoulded openings—stakes a claim of lineage through Lutyens to the Mughals.

The other non-Delhiite genius of that generation, B.V. Doshi, has also left his mark on Delhi, though thankfully not through his earliest projects. Having worked in Le Corbusier's office in Paris as a young man, Doshi contracted a particularly virulent strain of Corbusitis, and as a result the graceful city of Ahmedabad is sadly disfigured by some monstrous exercises in the brutalist style. In 1965, Doshi described architecture as 'an art which organises, co-ordinates and orders life by its function of providing enclosure so that human beings may lead a wholesome existence'—a spine-chilling example of the moralizing and social determinism of the modern movement. Nobody today wants to be taught how to live by their built environment.

Certainly not the students of the National Institute of Fashion Technology. Luckily, by the time Doshi came to Delhi to design their campus in 1994, his obsession with the shibboleths and forms of modernism was beginning to subside. The building is marked by an interest in a variety of surface textures (no longer just rough concrete), and centres on a sunken garden that is made in the form of an ancient stepwell. It is a shame that this space is not more popular with the students. Fearful of falling and breaking their ankles, they prefer to congregate on the institute's front steps on the main road. But this neglected garden is a genuine gesture of respect for a past that Doshi was once so eager to escape.

Meanwhile, Delhi's resident architects were pursuing similar lines. Achyut Kanvinde's National Science Centre (1985) has chhatri-like turrets and a Steinian approach to integrating plants. C.P. Kukreja put away his stack of Kahnian bricks and reminded us—in a commercial office tower called Amba Deep (1990)—that it is possible to cover the exterior of a building in coloured mosaic tiles and geometric patterns. It is a spectacular building, not least because it marks a complete volte-face from all the modernist rhetoric about the iniquity of ornament. It is a sort of sultanate tower for our times. Romi Khosla, in his graceful design for a school for the Spastics Society (1993), seems to be reaching even further back, playing with the lines of ancient rock-cut *chaitya* halls.

The most overt use of a culturally rooted visual imagery is in the Baha'i House of Worship, popularly called the Lotus Temple, designed by the Iranian architect Fariborz Sahba in the early 1980s. As is well known, Baha'i is a syncretic faith that draws on a broad range of different religious traditions. But if its ideas are inclusive, its iconography is not. There is a marked reluctance to include in its temples any forms or symbols that are specific to another religion. Thus no idols are permitted, no paintings, no music and no architectural ornament that refers to sacred traditions of the past. The only specific positive requirement is that the building must have nine sides, to reflect the pluralism of the faith's sources.

All of this presents a bit of a challenge to an architect. The temple must have nine sides and must obviously appear suitably sacred but must not resemble any specific religious prototype. Fariborz Sahba's solution was to select a form—that of the lotus flower—that is at once natural and redolent of India's ancient culture. The lotus is employed in the art of several of India's religious traditions, making its sacred associations generic rather than specific. Sahba's giant lotus building is composed of twenty-seven interlocking marble-clad petals, surrounded by pools, with almost no other embellishment. It appears both ancient and modern, a Taj Mahal revisited. The coincidental slight resemblance to the Sydney Opera House may be unfortunate but is perhaps more apparent to foreign than to local eyes. Since it was inaugurated in 1986, the Lotus Temple has been visited by over 100 million people from all over the world. On average it receives up to 10,000 visitors per day. Many are tourists, curious to see a famous modern monument; but from the spike in numbers on Hindu festival days we may infer that—despite the lack of imagery—many more see it as another prominent sacred shrine in the vast bowl-like arena of Delhi. It is a building which settles comfortably into and reflects Delhi's historical and cultural layers, on account of its own layered and segmented structure, and because its starkly modern aesthetic presents to our gaze a form that has been plucked from India's ancient past.

The city's most prestigious architectural practice is that of Raj Rewal. One of his best known early projects is the Asian Games Village (1982) inside Siri Fort. The yellow reconstituted stone cladding, the complex rectilinear geometry and the close-knit, pedestrianized planning all consciously evoke the pattern of traditional Rajasthani towns like Jaisalmer. Of course it is partly a matter of perception. A decade after the Asian Games Village was completed, its residents were interviewed and asked for their views on its use of traditional Indian planning principles. 'Nonsense,' they retorted, 'it's not Indian, it's modern. For one thing, it's tidy. If you want to see what a traditional Indian town is like you have to go to Old Delhi.' You can't please everyone. But the historians and critics were persuaded that this project heralded a genuine Indian revival.

If there was any note of doubt, it was only about the relevance of Jaisalmer as a model for Delhi. In subsequent projects, Rewal tackled this head on. In place of the yellow reconstituted stone cladding, he used red and buff panels, to imitate the Dholpur sandstone that had been used by Lutyens and Baker and, before them, by the Mughals, in such conspicuous Delhi landmarks as Humayun's tomb. Buildings such as the Indian Institute of Immunology (1983) and the SCOPE office complex (completed 1989) attribute and affirm a two-tone colour coding for the city. The SCOPE complex seems to proclaim its descent from Humayun's tomb, not just through its colour but by its scale, its use of the octagon in planning and the domed chhatris. Lutyens too—despite his protest—had used chhatris, and Rewal's repetition of the gesture establishes their place in the permanent lexicon of Delhi.

Of the very many projects that Rewal has completed since—large and small, in Delhi and elsewhere including abroad—one more merits special mention: the office for the World Bank in Lodi Estate (1996), because here too he clearly turned to the city's Mughal architecture for inspiration, but this time on a different scale. The articulation of the façades around the central courtyard and the detailing of their stonework with overhanging *jharokhas*, evoke less the grand imperial gesture of a mausoleum and more the domestic scale and intimacy of a Shahjahanabad haveli.

In pursuing this mediation between tradition and modernity, architects were attempting to define a new Indian identity. And in this pursuit, architecture did not stand alone but expressed a wider spirit of the times. The 1980s was also the era of the Festivals of India when art and crafts enthusiasts joined hands with museum curators to reconsider how India should depict itself in exhibitions held in Britain, France, Russia and America. It was also the era of 'ethnic chic' when leading experts on India's regional textile traditions would turn up at Delhi parties wearing ghaghras, or peasant skirts. In many domains, folk design was seized on as a source of inspiration because it was seen as authentic: Indian and yet alive, not hauled from the obscurity of a museum store.

These matters were debated at length with great passion. Today, people in Delhi seem less anxious about what constitutes Indian identity. This is not because the debate was concluded and the answers agreed, but because they are more preoccupied with other things, and especially with the scope and speed of changes brought on by the liberalization of the Indian economy, a process that began in 1991.

SCOPE office complex, designed by Raj Rewal, completed in 1989; photograph by the author, 1992

The State Trading Corporation building, designed by Raj Rewal in 1989; photographed by Madan Mahatta

The decades of liberalization have transformed Delhi (and other Indian cities) socially and culturally in a variety of ways, some of which are profound and some are trivial but a part of everyday life. Before liberalization, for example, the only way of getting a telephone connection was through the state-owned company, and the waiting time for most people was twenty-five years. Even if you bribed your way up the queue, your children would have grown up and migrated without ever having phoned home. If you wanted to speak to someone abroad, you had to visit the Central Telegraph Office to book an ISTD call. Nowadays every farmer in the hinterland has a mobile phone and can call to check prices to decide whether it is worthwhile coming to market.

Back in the 1970s, there were not too many cars on Delhi's streets, and those that were there were mostly of the same model: the stately if curvy Ambassador, a revamped Morris Oxford, as everyone knows, made by Hindustan Motors. Owning one was a tremendous status symbol, and even today there remain a few politicians and senior bureaucrats who use one as a badge of pride. The breakthrough for normal folk came with the launch of the Maruti 800. Light and inexpensive, it enabled many more drivers to take to the roads. Now there is a wide array of different models, both Indian and foreign, and a vast increase in number—around a million cars at present with a similar number of other vehicles. As a result, many arterial roads are in a state of permanent gridlock. People prefer to use the rapidly expanding Metro rail system that rests on vast pylons rising above the roads.

The Metro is certainly the best way to reach the outermost parts of the National Capital Region. If you are on your way to dinner in Gurgaon, you might like to pick up a bottle of wine en route. Easily done nowadays. Back in the 1980s, it was like trying to buy wine in the reign of Muhammad bin Tughluq.

In January 2007, the International Network for Traditional Building, Architecture and Urbanism (INTBAU) held a conference in Delhi. As its name suggests, INTBAU promotes traditional values in planning and design. In the West this often means supporting the revival of classicism, which was supposedly expunged by modernism. Its patron is the Prince of Wales. Coming to Delhi was about trying to see if there were like-minded people among the architectural profession here: people ready to shake off the shackles of the modern movement and embrace some inspiration from the past. Of course they were about twenty years too late; they would have done better if they had come in the 1980s when such forces were indeed stirring. One of the keynote speakers was Leon Krier, an architect and theorist who has worked for Prince Charles (he made the master plan for the new town of Poundbury in Dorset). With great passion and verve, he delivered a speech he had obviously given many times before, sketching a vision in which we all live in houses made of brick and stucco, no building is ever more than four storeys tall, every town is medium sized and yet we all have everything we need—schools, hospitals, libraries, banks, shops, the lot—within easy walking distance. His drawings depicting all this show pretty rows of varied houses and avenues of pollarded trees, like something off a biscuit tin.

I was assigned the unenviable task of taking Krier and a busload of other delegates on a tour of Gurgaon (where I happen to live) in order to inspect this current example of Indian urban development in action. Coming at the end of a long and tiring day—and timed to coincide with the rush hour—this jaunt did not go well. On crossing the border into Haryana, I pointed to the glittering DLF 'Gateway Tower', a twelve-storey office block designed by the famous, if controversial, architect Hafeez Contractor. Though completed and in use, the tower then still had clustering around its base the shacks of the migrant workers who had constructed it. They have since moved on of course, but such scenes are common in Gurgaon and visibly convey the social inequalities that the city's very growth embodies. Krier was appalled. Not by the squalor but by the design of the tower, as its height and glass sheath are affronts against tradition. In his speech he made sure everyone knew how low he rated my skills as a guide and described the Gateway Tower as 'a gigantic lipstick'. I'm not sure what he has against lipstick. We Gurgaon people call it the 'ship building' because the outline of its plan is shaped like a boat. But 'lipstick' makes me like it more . . . makes it almost sexy.

The guest of honour at the conference was Raj Rewal. The distinguished architect spent an hour showing pictures and discussing some of his completed and ongoing projects. Rewal was the obvious and perfect choice for this role. A guiding force in the Indian revival movement of the 1980s described earlier, he has remained true to its spirit. He employs modern technologies and design methods but infuses each work with a distinctively Indian spirit. Typically, he takes a traditional motif or pattern and reinvents it, adapting it to a new scale or purpose. The transformation leaves you with a sense of connectedness, but also intrigues you as you try to figure out how he does it. The trouble is, he is not very good at describing this, or explaining his methods. It is not that, like a conjuror, he won't reveal his tricks. He just can't. His approach to the past is instinctive and visual, not verbal. He just shows you what he has done and expects you to get it.

Well, Leon Krier wasn't having any of it. As soon as Rewal finished, Krier leapt to his feet, ostensibly to thank him, but took everyone by surprise by commenting acidly, 'You aren't a traditional architect! You're a modernist!' Now, in Krier's vocabulary this is not a compliment. It's like calling someone a barbarian. The irony is, of course, that he is right (not about the barbarian bit): Rewal is indeed a modernist. One of the buildings that made his name was an industrial exhibition space, the Hall of Nations, at Pragati Maidan. Inaugurated in 1972, it was condemned as having outlived its usefulness and was suddenly and surreptitiously demolished in 2017—to the horror of architects and conservationists who mourned this loss of a 'heritage' structure. Since that term was used, let us be clear that the heritage in question is India's post-Independence modern movement. The design principle employed in the Hall of Nations was the space frame. Indeed Rewal originally proposed to build it in steel. On finding the cost of steel to be prohibitively high, he switched to concrete, as the major cost in concrete construction is the labour force required to make the formwork, and Indian labour is cheap. As a space frame made in concrete, the Hall of Nations was actually something of an anomaly, as well as an exercise in the brutalist aesthetic. Of course, depending on taste, those are not reasons not to mourn it. Rewal's many later projects are very different in aesthetic, but they are no less modern.

Rewal seemed rather nonplussed by Krier's attack, as well he might be. I mean, one's colleagues invite one to be a guest of honour and give one a platform, and then some angry foreigner delivers what is obviously meant as an insult, but one is not sure quite how. Rewal's softly muttered retort sounded very like, 'Well, I'd rather be a modernist than a fuddy-duddy!'

So Leon Krier is not going to find his architectural paradise, his land of innocence, in any place designed by Raj Rewal. Neither will he find it in Gurgaon. Cyber City, as seen from the expressway, looks like a set design for a Star Wars movie, like a film-maker's idea of an intergalactic space station. The city develops according to the dictates of market forces, with no coherent master plan. In the west, it has sped down the NH8 as far as Manesar, halfway to the border with Rajasthan. To the south, it has swept over farmlands and stands poised to engulf Badshahpur. It is strong on resources—it has some excellent schools and hospitals—but is poor in infrastructure. Its roads in particular are not well maintained—an imbalance which reflects the dominance of the private sector. None of its architecture looks back towards Delhi, but outwards, towards Dubai and Singapore. It has an enormous wholesale market for marble, brought straight from the quarries of Rajasthan; but developers proudly boast of using not this but marble imported from Italy. Its whole futuristic promise is based on a denial of its location.

So how is one to respond to this megacity? Can one make any connection between today's urban sprawl and the earliest parts of Delhi? Shall we join hands with the fuddy-duddies and decry the destructive march of the modern era? Not me. It may seem far-fetched to look at a map of Gurgaon and see its embryo in the courtyard of the Quwwatu'l-Islam. But the story retold in these pages is of a city that keeps making itself anew and larger. Each of the successive cities of Delhi was once a brash interloper, embarrassing its older predecessors as it jostled for space and increased the scale. Today, we may look with nostalgic pleasure at the quiet and quaint avenues of central New Delhi, the Lutyens Bungalow Zone; but in the 1920s it was all brand new, with parts half-finished, and all laid out on a scale that made Old Delhi look like a model in a museum. But Old Delhi too was new and a grand imperial city in its day, as you can still see in descriptions by eyewitnesses like François Bernier. Gurgaon lacks the clear shape and order of its predecessors, but it marks no break in their purpose. It is just the next surge. And it won't be the last.

Suggested Routes

Each of the following routes could be covered in half a day—a period that may be abbreviated or lengthened according to the time available. Visitors to the city who have very limited time are advised to prioritize the first four routes. The remaining five are listed in geographical sequence, roughly from north to south. I have not included maps of the routes quite simply because no one any longer uses a book for information that is more conveniently found on a mobile phone. These routes are just stage one of a plan: they point to clusters of sites that are discussed in the book, which can conveniently be visited in a single trip. These routes are not conceived as walks: in every case a car or public transport is required to get to the starting point and (with the exception of the first and third) to get between the various sites included.

Shahjahanabad: Red Fort and Jami Masjid

The easiest way to reach Shahjahanabad, the old city of Delhi, is by the Metro (Yellow and Violet Lines). Approached by road, it seems cut off and remote. This was partly deliberate. Despite some token lines of connectivity, New Delhi was not planned to include it. The old city was then seen as insanitary and best avoided. Today, it feels like a different world from New Delhi, and from what it once was. The events of 1857 and 1947 had a profound demographic impact, with the expulsion or departure of large sections of the Muslim elites. And with modernization in the post-Independence era, the non-Muslim elites have left too. Owning a grand haveli in the old city, which had once been so fashionable, began to seem more like an embarrassment. Maintaining one, and sustaining an elegant lifestyle within it, became difficult in that increasingly congested space. Far better to abandon it in favour of a bungalow—or later an apartment—in one of the spacious new colonies of south Delhi. The haveli, if not torn down, would be closed up, or let out as storage space, or divided up among shopkeepers and other tenants. The city remains a frantically busy commercial hub, but it has lost its elite status, certainly as a place to live in. The core of the old city—known as Delhi 6 after its postal district number—is depicted in Bollywood movies as some quaint netherworld in which lovable rogues lead lives of misadventure, but where the built environment somehow imbues everything with a sense of reality and integrity.

It doesn't look like that from the real worlds of Connaught Place or the southern colonies: it just looks messy, dilapidated and crowded. Neither does it look particularly old. There are some surviving old havelis as well as mosques and madrasas, but the majority of the original, Mughal-era buildings have been replaced. What does survive is the street plan. As in the City of London, most individual buildings have been replaced, but on the same footprint, leaving the layout undisturbed. Not only the main thoroughfares, even the narrow winding lanes follow the routes that they did when the city was first developed.

The Lal Qila, or Red Fort (pp. 68–78), is a UNESCO World Heritage site but it is not well maintained. It is hard to get a sense, on the ground, of the original overall design concept, as planned by the principal architect of the Red Fort, Ustad Ahmad Lahauri (who was also the main architect of the Taj Mahal). But the fort is well worth visiting for some magnificent component parts including the Diwan-i-Am, with its marble throne *baldachino* (or canopy), and the Diwan-i-Khas. The recently revamped site museums do little to assist an understanding of the architecture, but do touch on some of the nationalist associations that the fort has acquired through its turbulent later history.

Netaji Subhash Road—named after Subhash Chandra Bose, who was instrumental in setting up the INA—separates the fort from the rest of the old city. But if you can negotiate your way across it, it is possible to walk down Chandni Chowk. That name, meaning 'moonlit square', is now given to the whole length of the road but originally referred to an open space at its midpoint. Sponsored by Jahanara, the emperor Shah Jahan's daughter, the octagonal chowk contained a pool to reflect the moon, and a hammam and a *sarai* for public use. One of the smaller alleys from the south side of Chandni Chowk, Dariba Kalan Road, leads to the north gate of the Jami Masjid (pp. 78–80). Gaining access to the mosque requires observing the dress code (no skirts or shorts) but is otherwise free. To plan your day, it is worth noting that non-Muslims are not allowed in during the lunchtime namaz or prayer.

Humayun's Tomb and Lodi Road

Top of my list of Delhi's must-see monuments is Humayun's tomb, which stands beyond the eastern end of Lodi Road, where it crosses the highway to Mathura (pp. 59–62). As you enter the garden from the west gate, instead of proceeding directly towards the tomb, it is worth turning right to walk through part of the garden and approach the tomb from the south, its proper entrance front. Inside the tomb, make sure to explore some of the corner chambers (accessed from the central hall) which contain some of the lesser graves. Outside on the platform, on the eastern side, you may be able to hear, if not glimpse, the railway line, just beyond the perimeter wall. The railway now runs where the river once did: like the Taj Mahal in Agra, this tomb once stood on the banks of the Yamuna.

Also on the platform, especially on the western side, there are seemingly random clusters of other graves. Why were some members of the imperial family buried inside the main building and others outside? It is impossible to be sure because we don't know who is who: none of the graves are marked with the names of those buried in them. Their position may reflect their status but my guess is that it has more to do with their orthodoxy. In strict Islamic tradition, nothing should cover the grave, certainly not a vast domed sepulchre. Having one's grave outside on the platform comes closer to observing that rule.

As you exit from the western gate, turn immediately left to pass through a small doorway into the Arab Sarai, where you will find the Afsarwala mosque and tomb (p. 63). Behind those buildings is the back of a grand gateway that enables you to leave the Arab Sarai and then re-enter Bu Halima's garden. On your left then is the entrance to Isa Khan's tomb and mosque (pp. 62–63).

Before leaving the area it is worth paying a visit to the Sunder Nagar nursery, on the northern side of the complex. Containing a handful of lesser tombs of the Mughal era, this area was once part of the larger necropolis. When New Delhi was under construction, it was turned into a nursery, for the many trees and plants required for the city's avenues and roundabouts, and it continued in that use until recently. But now the Aga Khan Trust for Culture (AKTC) has taken it in hand, restoring the buildings and laying out new gardens and landscaping in a modern Mughal idiom. At the time of writing, the AKTC is also constructing an interpretation centre at the entrance to the whole complex.

The excellent work of the AKTC, conducted over many years, has restored several parts of the necropolis and has reconnected them into an integrated whole. Even they, however, cannot undo the effect of the modern road layout, which severs Humayun and his immediate neighbours from the Sufi saint next to whom they wished to be buried, Nizamuddin Auliya (pp. 63–64). Founded in the early fourteenth century, his dargah lies at the heart of the old urban village of Nizamuddin, and can be reached by lanes leading from the eastern end of Lodi Road. Entering the dargah, you pass by the restored *baoli* or stepwell, built by his devotees to the fury of the sultan (p. 31). The actual tomb (or mazar) of the saint was often rebuilt or embellished by devotees; in its present form it dates from the nineteenth century. Within the precinct are the graves of two of his prominent devotees, of different eras: Amir Khusrau (who was the saint's contemporary) and Princess Jahanara (who lived three centuries later and was responsible for Chandni Chowk). Just outside are the tombs of Ataga Khan and of his son, the elegant Chaunsath Khamba (pp. 66–67).

Halfway down the Lodi Road, one comes across a startling juxtaposition of early and modern architecture: sultanate-era tombs within a stone's throw of some of the most experimental buildings of the mid-twentieth century. The Sayyid and Lodi period tombs of the Lodi Gardens (pp. 41–49) are among the finest and best preserved pre-Mughal buildings in Delhi. And the pleasure of visiting them is enhanced by the garden setting even if its form is unhistorical: the gardens were laid out in the picturesque manner by the British in 1936 and updated with quirky modernist lamp posts and fountains in the 1960s.

Hemming the garden in on its eastern side are some institutional buildings of more recent times. The India International Centre (IIC) and the Ford Foundation are two examples of the innovative and delightful early work of the architect Joseph Allen Stein (p. 125). A later and larger work emanating from the same office is the vast and sprawling Habitat Centre (1988–93), on the far side of the road, which houses art galleries and various bodies connected with the building trade. Its huge meandering courtyard is made to feel intimate, and the light is dappled, by the screens suspended high overhead.

Because of the clustering of these buildings, professors and students of architecture refer to the area affectionately as 'Steinabad'. But Stein is not the only modern architect represented here. Tibet House (1974, next door to the Habitat Centre) is one of those exercises in Le Corbusian brutalism by Shiv Nath Prasad (p. 122), though its original starkness and internationalism are mollified by the later painting of the exterior in bright colours inspired by Tibetan art. The office of the World Bank (1996) that is tucked away by the annexe to the IIC is a fine example of the work of Delhi's leading architect, Raj Rewal (p. 130). Nearby is the India Islamic Cultural Centre (S.K. Das and others, completed 2006) whose detached jalis and intricate mosaic ornament present a post-modern version of traditional Islamic design. To get a sense of the spacious planning and functional design of the housing colonies that were built in the mid-twentieth century, just before and after Independence, it is worth exploring the Lodi Estate (opposite the IIC) and the adjacent, more upmarket Golf Links.

At the western end of Lodi Road, we return to the Mughal period (though to a later phase of it) with the tomb of Safdarjang (p. 85).

The Qutb Minar and Mehrauli

The Qutb Minar and the mosque to which it is attached, the Quwwatu'l-Islam, are among the oldest stone structures built by a settled Muslim power in India, having been begun in the closing years of the twelfth century. Their early date, as much as their prominence and beauty—not to mention their status as a

UNESCO World Heritage site—lend them an iconic status in Delhi's architectural landscape (pp. 8–18 and, for later additions, pp. 26–29).

With so many phases of building, it is hard to make sense of the complex until you have seen it all. So here is one suggested route through the maze. Follow the curving entrance path to the left and then turn right to head first for the central courtyard of the mosque. After exploring that (and the iron pillar) leave the courtyard through the north-west corner of the ruined prayer hall to visit the tomb of Iltutmish. From there, take the path that goes back behind the mosque to the madrasa, and from there into the southern extension of the mosque built by Iltutmish. At the far end of that stands the Qutb Minar and behind it the Alai Darwaza. Exit through the latter so you can see its fine southern façade. Then (facing the gate) turn right and take the flight of steps up into the garden, where you will find Robert Smith's folly and Gordon Sanderson's sundial.

Sanderson was a brilliant young archaeologist who, after a short stint studying the Islamic architecture of Cairo, joined the Archaeological Survey of India. In 1912, he was deputed to assess the viability of entrusting the design of New Delhi to Indian rather than British architects; his report suggesting that it could was published but also trashed by the government (see p. 105). At the same time, he studied the historic monuments of Delhi to consider the likely impact of the construction of the new city on them. With the outbreak of World War I, he sailed to England to sign up. On the voyage he fell in love. On disembarking he immediately married, conceived a child, was despatched to the front and within weeks was killed. Much of his work came to light only recently when his grandson (who of course never knew him) inherited his papers from his mother (Sanderson's child), recognized their significance and made them available. At the time of his death, Sanderson's colleagues in the ASI erected the sundial in his memory. It is a short walk from the sundial back to the exit.

The village of Mehrauli, to the south-west of the Qutb complex, is dense and congested. The tomb of Adham Khan (p. 65) stands at the north end of the village and is most easily reached by the road that runs behind the Qutb complex. From this point too one can climb up onto the top of a surviving section of the old wall of the Lal Kot, the fort built by the Rajputs. Up there, one is above the level of the tree canopy and the modern urban context suddenly vanishes. It is like looking at the plains of Delhi in a print by the Daniells.

The Hauz-i-Shamsi, the tank built by Iltutmish in 1230, lies at the southern end of the village and is best approached from a turning off the Mehrauli–Gurgaon Road. The dargah of Qutb Sahib, the Sufi saint, is towards the centre and can only be reached on foot (p. 23). It is fascinating as an active shrine, but women are not permitted to enter the enclosure where the saint lies buried.

Between the village and the bypass (to the east) is a large area, once a suburb of the oldest city, now mostly fenced in and defined as the 'Mehrauli Archaeological Park'. Somewhat reminiscent of the Lodi Gardens (though less well-tended), this area is a mixture of gardens, orchards, nurseries and woodland, dotted with historic monuments, including the Jamali-Kamali mosque and tomb and the tomb of Quli Khan (pp. 54–55, 66).

A few hundred yards to the west of the Jamali-Kamali mosque is the Rajon-ki-Bain, a multi-tiered stepwell. At one end a flight of steps leads down into the water, while on the three other sides galleries and apartments line the retaining walls. A small mosque on a connecting platform contains an inscription that states it was built in 1506, in the reign of Sikander Lodi. But the well might be older. As a form of underground architecture, stepwells are often dramatic but this one has an especially arresting composition. It was probably made for the benefit of the general public, a source of supply of water for domestic use; with apartments added as cool places to rest during the hottest months.

On the far side of the bypass, near the junction with the Badarpur Road, a small square tomb, said to be that of one 'Azim Khan' (about whom nothing is known) crowns a rocky eminence. In form it is like many other late Lodi or early Mughal tombs, but its spectacular location enhances its impact wonderfully. The next hillock to the south is used in a similar way to a very different purpose. Now called Ahimsa Sthal or 'seat of non-violence', it is surmounted by a huge modern statue of Mahavir, the last of the twenty-four Jain Thirthankaras, often considered the founder of the religion, carved in polished granite from Karnataka. The saint directs his stony gaze northwards towards the busy city, but with the archaeological park to his left and a patch of green-belt to his right, his hilltop throne is surrounded by a carpet of greenery, and the sides of the hill are clad with a well-kept garden.

Heading south towards Gurgaon, the bypass ascends a ridge, beyond which a branch road leads to the former village of Chhatarpur, now dominated by a vast modern temple complex. The Chhatarpur temple, spread over sixty acres, is one of the largest in India and is always thronged with multitudes of devotees. The main shrine is dedicated to the goddess Katyayani, an avatar of Durga, and includes—beside the normal image chamber—a fully furnished sitting room and a bedroom for her personal use. The temple was founded in 1974 by Baba Sant Nagpalji (d. 1988) whose samadhi or cremation site lies within the complex. There are more than twenty other temples besides, all built of stone and mostly in a conservative south Indian style, thus showing the tradition to be alive (if a touch ossified) and as exuberant as ever.

Rajpath and Janpath

One way to catch a glimpse of Rashtrapati Bhavan—the former Viceroy's House (pp. 105–109)—is to drive up the slope of Raisina hill between the Secretariats, hop out while the driver lingers under the watchful gaze of the police (no parking is permitted) and peer between the bars of the handsome iron gates. If you cannot see much detail from this distance, you can at least get a sense of the palace's profile and its relation to the other buildings, including the curious way in which the slope blocks the view as you approach, so that it seems to disappear, only to pop up again when you reach the summit. Edwin Lutyens, who did not foresee this effect—the result of Herbert Baker's insistence that the Secretariats should stand on the crest, not at the foot, of the hill—called it his Bakerloo. He felt it marred the design. He didn't want mystery, he wanted dominance. The critic Robert Byron described the palace as 'a slap on the face of democracy'. He meant it as a compliment.

Now the official residence of the President of the Indian Republic, the palace is open to the public on application. Visitors are given a short tour. This is well worth doing to see the details of the stone carving, and the grand apartments such as the Durbar Hall and the Ballroom. The main staircase is contained in an open courtyard, topped by a coving that makes the sky look like a brilliant blue ceiling; it is quite the cleverest neoclassical staircase since the vestibule of the Laurentian Library. Another thing that is alone worth seeing is the fine Qajjar-period painting of Fath Ali Shah out hunting, which is stuck on the ceiling of the former State Ballroom (now called the Ashoka Hall). This was not a part of Lutyens's plan; he had intended restrained decorations that would not detract from the architecture. But Lady Willingdon had other ideas. In 1932, she found the painting in the India Office (it seems to have been presented to the Prince Regent in 1814) and had it shipped out to India, where she engaged Tomasso Colonnello and a team of Indian assistants to transform the Ballroom into a Persian-themed extravaganza, with Fath Ali Shah riding overhead.

One may approach Baker's Secretariat buildings—North and South Blocks (pp. 106–109)—closely enough to admire the detailing, but not enter them, since they are still occupied by the principal ministries. The former Council House, now the Parliament building—down the slope and away to the left—is even more strictly guarded, with good reason, as it has been the target of a (foiled) terrorist attack in recent times.

India Gate (p. 108) sits at the centre of an octagon defined by a road that was originally called Princes Place, because the adjoining plots were assigned to various leading maharajas to enable them to build palaces in the new capital. The clustering of leading maharajas here was meant to signal their participation in the empire. Since Independence their houses have all been acquired by the state and assigned new functions. The most elegant, Hyderabad House, designed by Lutyens, is now reserved for entertaining visiting heads of state (though spurned by one US President, allegedly because he was told that both the security and the cheeseboard were better at the Maurya Sheraton). Baroda House is now the headquarters of the northern railways board; Patiala House is the Delhi district court; while Bikaner House is the office of the Rajasthan tourism board and a venue for cultural events.

At the south-east corner is Jaipur House, designed by Geoffrey and Francis Blomfield (p. 114). This elegant mansion, and the extension built in 2009 by A.R. Ramanathan and Snehanshu Mukherjee, together house the National Gallery of Modern Art, the nation's largest and finest collection of painting and sculpture dating from the nineteenth century and later. Among the leading modern Indian artists whose works are particularly well represented here are Abanindranath Tagore, Amrita Sher-Gil, Jamini Roy and Ramkinker Baij.

Earlier phases of Indian art are exhibited at the National Museum, located at the intersection of Rajpath with Janpath, the north-south perpendicular road, formerly called Queensway, which bisects Rajpath at its midpoint. The purpose-built structure (inaugurated in 1960) is not handsome and is not well maintained, and a visit is not the aesthetic delight that it ought to be. The vast and magnificent collection of stone sculpture—comprising mostly idols and temple fragments—is unimaginatively displayed, with pieces glued on to pedestals with minimal labelling. This may be acceptable to specialists who already know what they are seeing, but it is unhelpful to anyone trying to get acquainted with India's most characteristic genre of art. The miniature paintings (Mughal, Rajasthani and Pahari) fare a little better, but only a small proportion of the collection is included. The other galleries—archaeology, anthropology, numismatics—are dispiriting, and there is far too little space in the textile gallery. The gift shop has improved after a makeover, but it still lacks books. There are too few publications on the museum's holdings. That's partly because there are too few staff to write them: half the curators' posts have been vacant for decades. Government institutions don't have to be like this.

Heading north up Janpath, after crossing over Rajpath, one passes the National Archives on the left (not open to the public) and another cultural institution on the right: the Indira Gandhi National Centre for the Arts (IGNCA). A centre for research that also promotes exhibitions, it is housed in two buildings that were meant to be temporary (an army mess dating from the 1930s, and an exhibition space hastily erected in the 1990s) and one that is incomplete. After its establishment in 1987, an international competition was held to produce a design for the many libraries and galleries that were projected to cover the sprawling campus. Amid numerous superb entries from architects from India and abroad, the selection committee chose a truly atrocious design by the American architect Ralph Lerner, and it is only a small consolation that just one of the buildings was constructed (and that too remains unfinished). Despite this, the IGNCA succeeds in publishing scholarly books and staging innovative exhibitions.

Further north up Janpath on the left is the Imperial, one of Delhi's grandest hotels, designed by Geoffrey Blomfield, in a streamlined Art Deco style. The hotel went into decline in the 1970s but has since been renovated with lush new interiors in a manner that is nostalgically reminiscent of the typical Indian club—a superior kind of Gymkhana. On the walls of the central corridor and the main reception rooms hang aquatints and engravings of Indian views, mainly by British artists from the Daniells to William Simpson: a veritable art gallery and one of the finest collections of such views to be found outside the British Library. The bar and the veranda cafe (named 1911, after the Delhi Durbar of that year) are also well worth a visit.

The modern building that looms opposite the Imperial, with some dangerous-looking cantilevers, was designed by Raj Rewal. It houses the Central Cottage Industries Emporium—the main government-run outlet for handicrafts. The eccentrically octagonal windows and stone cladding are meant to evoke the architectural forms of older parts of Delhi (see p. 132).

Round the corner in Tolstoy Marg is one of those older parts though with an equally startling geometry: the Jantar Mantar is one of the astronomical observatories of Maharaja Sawai Jai Singh II of Jaipur (p. 84). When it was built in the early eighteenth century, the land belonged to Jaipur. Indeed a large swathe of what is now New Delhi once belonged to Jaipur and had to be purchased from Sawai Jai Singh II's later successor, Maharaja Sawai Madho Singh II, when the city was laid out. A little to the west, on Baba Kharak Singh Marg, is a Hanuman temple of which the Jaipur maharajas were the original patrons; and a Sikh gurdwara known as Bangla Sahib—so called because the founder, Guru Har Krishan, was permitted to take up residence in the compound of what was then the 'lord's bungalow', the Delhi residence of the Jaipur ruler. Although these two sacred sites are visited by many pilgrims daily, their historical associations are largely forgotten, as new layers of meaning take over. In the same way, few now visit the Jantar Mantar in order to study eighteenth-century astronomy. They go there because (like India Gate) it has become a site of protest—in this case largely political. The Jantar Mantar is where you go if you want to agitate or fast to show your disapproval of the government. So Delhi's Jaipur connection is most visible not here but at our route's starting point: in the elegant Jaipur Column that stands proudly in the forecourt in front of Rashtrapati Bhavan, donated as a reminder of the previous landlord.

Kashmiri Gate and Beyond

There is a cluster of historic buildings in the far northern part of the old city, once the focal point of the early British settlement (in the first half of the nineteenth century, before the 1857 Revolt). From in front of the Red Fort, if you take the main road northwards, and pass under the railway line, you come onto Lothian Road. On an island in the middle of the road is what remains of the gateways of the British magazine. The magazine itself was blown up by its British defenders in 1857, to prevent it falling into the hands of the sepoy forces taking control of Delhi. Continue up Lothian Road and you come, on the left, to what is currently the office of the Election Commission, but built as the original St Stephen's College, in 1890, designed by Samuel Swinton Jacob. The consulting engineer to the princely state of Jaipur, Jacob developed an architectural practice that promoted a revivalist style and—at least in Rajasthan—exemplified an admirable method of collaboration with local craftsmen. At the end of his career he served briefly as an unwanted adviser on Indian architecture to Lutyens. This early building is not his best work. In fact, it's rather grim. But it shows how Jacob, in Delhi, tried to respond to Lodi-era monuments (just as he responded, more successfully, to living local traditions when in Jaipur).

Further up and obliquely across, as the road opens up into a square, is St James's Church, built in 1835 by James Skinner, and designed by Robert Smith (of Qutb-cupola fame, p. 14). It is an elegant neoclassical building, with a Greek cross plan. Among the graves in the graveyard are those of two British residents of Delhi: William Fraser, who was murdered in 1835 (and his grave was vandalized in 1857—he was unpopular in some quarters) and Thomas Metcalfe, who died in 1853. St James's was the most important church for the early British community in Delhi. Its patron, James Skinner, was an Anglo-Indian who battled against prejudice to become a powerful ally of the British.

From the church it is a short walk to Kashmiri Gate, the northern gate of the old city, and the point at which forces under Brigadier Nicholson entered to recapture Delhi on 14 September 1857. It still bears the scars of that encounter. After the event it was not restored but preserved as a sort of shrine to British courage in the face of horror.

Outside the gate, if you can get past the bus terminal and the busy Metro station and cross Lala Hardev Sahai Marg, and enter Sham Nath Marg, you will find, on the left, the cemetery in which Nicholson is buried and, on the right, the remains of the Qudsia

Bagh, a garden palace built in 1748 for the favourite queen (a former dancing girl) of Muhammad Shah Rangila. Today, there is just a gateway, a *baradari* and a mosque. Much of the rest seems to have been destroyed in 1857, not because it was expressly targeted but simply because it stood in the line of fire between the sepoy forces defending the city walls and the British forces assembled on the ridge to the north-west.

If you proceed onto the ridge, you can visit the Mutiny Memorial, a Gothic spire erected in 1863 with a plaque commemorating those who fell on the British side, and a postscript, added in 1972, honouring the heroism of their adversaries. Beyond it lies the campus of Delhi University, which includes the home of St Stephen's College since 1939, designed by Walter George (p. 115).

Central New Delhi—North

The route starts at the Anglican cathedral (the Cathedral Church of the Redemption, on Church Road on the north side of Rashtrapati Bhavan, p. 112) and proceeds north, via North Avenue and a section of Mother Teresa Crescent, to the original post office, the Gol Dak-khana and the Catholic Cathedral of the Sacred Heart (p. 112). Continuing up Baba Kharak Singh Marg, you pass both Bangla Sahib Gurdwara and the Hanuman Mandir (p. 154), to New Delhi's original main shopping centre, Connaught Place (designed by Robert Tor Russell, 1920s, p. 115). The fortunes of Connaught Place come and go. Situated between the ceremonial buildings of the central vista and the old city, it was conceived as the new commercial hub. All the smartest shops, restaurants and cinemas were here. With the establishment of many district markets across the city in the late twentieth century, CP began to lose its pre-eminence and shine. It started to look shabby. But restoration work and the coming of the Metro (there is a major station under its central garden) have restored its fortunes. Among the glittering showrooms of international retail chains, some of the original establishments—coffee houses and pastry shops—are still there, burnished but otherwise unchanged, allowing one to indulge in a little 1930s nostalgia, if that is to your taste.

Leaving CP by Kasturba Gandhi Marg, one comes to the British Council (Charles Correa, 1992) just before the junction with Tolstoy Marg. To the east (and reached by either Barakhamba Road or Firoz Shah Road) is Mandi House, another region with a cluster of arts institutions in exceptional buildings including Rabindra Bhavan (Habib Rahman), Triveni Kala Sangam (Joseph Allen Stein), Shri Ram Arts Centre (Shiv Nath Prasad) and Himachal Bhavan (Satish Grover). Together these buildings chart the development of Indian design from the impact of Corbusian modernism in the 1960s to more regionalist approaches that followed (pp. 122–127). The institutions they house also feature prominently in the present life of the city.

Central New Delhi—South

The route starts at Birla House, the site of Mahatma Gandhi's assassination, located on Tees January Marg, between Akbar and Aurangzeb Roads. Though structurally little has changed, this fine house is now run as a memorial museum. It is a tough call to build a museum collection around a man who left behind so little in terms of material possessions as Gandhi did; but there is a display of historical photographs and (upstairs) some interactive models that illustrate aspects of Gandhian thought. Outside in the garden you can trace his last steps up to the spot where Nathuram Godse barged his way through the crowd to shoot the Mahatma at point-blank range.

The route proceeds via Akbar Road (with glimpses of New Delhi's famous officials' bungalows) to the Indira Gandhi Memorial (her former residence, now a museum) in Safdarjang Road; and from there to Teen Murti Bhavan (built as the residence of the commander-in-chief, later used by Nehru and now a memorial museum to him). From there we proceed south-west into the diplomatic quarter, Chanakyapuri, and glimpse from outside some selected embassies which make, or attempt, major architectural statements, including the US Embassy (Edward Durrell Stone, 1958); the Belgian Embassy (Satish Gujral, 1983, p. 124); the French Embassy school (Raj Rewal, 1984); and the Pakistani High Commission (Karl Heinz, 1963).

We will pass over the British High Commission, which is a disgrace. The country of Inigo Jones, Christopher Wren and Edwin Lutyens apparently forgot the persuasive and political power of architecture when it came to representing themselves in the capital of its former empire. Almost within sight of the dome of what had been Viceroy's House, they erected the dreariest group of buildings that post-war Britain could muster.

The loveliest is the US Embassy. How it came to be so exquisite is a story told by the essayist Tom Wolfe. The architect, Edward Durrell Stone, first made his name as a committed modernist of the most minimalist order. His Museum of Modern Art in New York (1939) is achingly ugly. But in 1953, on a flight from New York to Paris, he found himself seated next to a woman named Maria, whom he described as 'explosively Latin'. Before they landed, he fell in love and proposed. But the lady was cautious. She didn't like his clothes and she didn't like his architecture. He vowed to change both. And thus it is that the American Embassy in Delhi has columns that taper towards the base so that they seem to stand on tiptoe like ballerinas; and they are ornamented with gold leaf. There are marble grilles and terrazzo tiling. He called it Taj Maria! The modernist purists were aghast. How could anyone be so vulgar? They excommunicated him. But he had got the girl.

Rajghat to the Lotus Temple

This route is a grand sweep down the whole eastern side of the city, using the Ring Road that follows the line of the Yamuna river. But Delhi's river is elusive. Though the city has been built and rebuilt on its bank many times, it is all but invisible to the casual visitor. In Agra, downstream, the same river seems always to be getting in the way, barring the path between you and your destination. But you can explore most of the places described in this book without so much as catching a glimpse of it. Partly this is because the historical Delhi (unlike Agra) does not straddle the river; it was built only on one side, the west bank, and the fickle, shallow-bedded river has changed its course and wandered away to the east, leaving the city remote and unwashed. Commuters from Noida, the modern satellite city on the eastern bank, cross the Yamuna daily, but for most it is just a name, a thing forgotten.

Even so, the river has played a role in iconic moments in the city's modern history. Mahatma Gandhi was assassinated on the afternoon of 30 January 1948, on the lawns of Birla House, the private home of one of his industrialist patrons, in the calm and elegant centre of Lutyens's New Delhi. But he was cremated (where else?) on the riverbank, just outside the old city. When kings or saints of the past were cremated a domed pavilion was raised to mark the spot, and this latter-day saint too has a memorial on his cremation ground, a simple and restrained affair without flourish or ornament, in keeping with his lifestyle. Designed by the architect Vanu G. Bhuta, it consists of a black marble platform surrounded by low stone walls. The Devanagari inscription on one end reads 'He Ram'—an invocation of the god Ram, and Gandhi's last words as he fell dying.

This spot is an inescapable port of call for visiting heads of state. Controversial throughout his political life, Mahatma Gandhi is uncontroversial in death as an exemplar of peace and reconciliation, venerated by leaders of all persuasions. Besides the politicians, about 10,000 other visitors come here daily. The cremation site is a suitable place to reflect on Gandhi's life and death by those who already know about him, but those wishing to learn might find it more instructive to visit the assassination spot, Birla House (p. 157).

The Ring Road that passes Rajghat, now officially called Mahatma Gandhi Road, leads south towards two riverside forts. The first is the Kotla built by Firuz Shah Tughluq in the fourteenth century, with its strange ziggurat surmounted by an imported Ashokan column, engraved with what was then an unreadable Brahmi inscription. This fort also contains a plain and ruined but handsomely proportioned mosque and an elaborate stepwell (p. 33).

The stone gateway that stands in the middle of the main road, just outside the Kotla on its western side, despite appearances, is not historically connected with it. It was built two centuries later as the northern gate of a city wall that enclosed—along with many buildings that are now lost—the next fort down the line, the Purana Qila. Developed by the early Mughals and the Sur dynasty (pp. 56–59), this stately if crumbling fort also once overlooked the river.

The walls of the Purana Qila provide a dramatic backdrop for the Delhi Zoo (the National Zoological Park) situated to its south. Developed in the 1950s with the help of expert guidance imported from Hungary, the zoo includes specimens of Bengal tiger, black bear, Indian rhinoceros, several species of deer and many brightly plumaged waterbirds such as painted storks. Like all zoos, it is a favourite place for family outings. Sandwiched between the zoo and the main road is a colony and market called Sunder Nagar, whose residents are serenaded through the night by the roars of lions and tigers.

Continuing south-east, past Humayun's tomb and Nizamuddin (see above, the section on Lodi Road), the Mathura Road eventually crosses the southern Outer Ring Road. A little to the west, towards Nehru Place, stand two remarkable temples, one ancient, the other modern. The first is the Kalkaji Mandir, among the most popular and oldest shrines in Delhi, which contains a self-fashioned or self-revealed image of the goddess Kali. The present building itself does not appear very old, two hundred years at most, but the antiquity of the shrine is a matter less of archaeology than of faith. Its origins lie less in history than in epic and legend since devotees believe that Lord Krishna and the Pandavas worshipped here before and after the battle of Kurukshetra. Many of today's pilgrims approach it with specific requests to lay before the goddess as the temple is also known as Manokamna Siddha Peetha, the 'desire-fulfilling shrine'.

Nearby is the undeniably modern Baha'i House of Worship, popularly known as the Lotus Temple, designed by the Iranian architect Fariborz Sahba and built in the 1980s (p. 128).

Hauz Khas to Tughluqabad

The route starts at Hauz Khas, the fourteenth-century madrasa complex by a lake built by Firuz Shah Tughluq, where the students dined so sumptuously (see pp. 35–36). The madrasa complex itself is entered through a gate at the end of the main road of the old village which clusters around the site and now houses a number of fashionable boutiques and restaurants. The lake is at a lower level and is approached separately, through the entrance to the deer park at the start of the village. The path around the lake and the gardens beyond it are a great place for a morning or evening stroll. So too are the woods on the far side of the deer park (reached by turning right inside its entry gate) which are dotted with tombs of the Lodi era, including a stately one known as Bagh-i-Alam.

Percy Brown wasn't wrong when he moaned about the profusion of Lodi tombs (p. 40), just a little spoilt and ungrateful. Perhaps as an art historian he felt burdened by the impossibility of writing about all of them. There are indeed a lot and they are very similar to one another, varying only in size and their state of preservation. But they add immensely to the rich tapestry of Delhi's past. The A-list monuments—the UNESCO World Heritage sites—are truly fantastic: we do our homework, we buy a ticket and we take a round. But it is a wonder of another kind to go for a walk in a wood and stumble across a fifteenth-century tomb, crumbling and lichen-covered, its inner chamber a home to feral dogs, its outer niches nesting places for parakeets. Maybe the resident flame-back woodpecker will put in an appearance, flickering gold briefly on a nearby tree. But the stone walls stand solid, and the dome resolutely raises its arc against the painfully shining sky. The view of it bursts upon you, to tell you that five hundred years ago, others came where you now walk, and built something to last—worthy to last—even if they themselves have not. The sheer frequency of this—for indeed, there are so many—is a part of what makes Delhi special.

People who live in Delhi can take such encounters for granted. It is just a perk of the real estate. They might string up a volleyball net in what was once its garden. Good for them! So long as they don't scratch their names on its walls. So long as they pause once in a while to consider how playing in the shadow of such buildings connects them with the past.

From Hauz Khas village, we head south on the main road (Aurobindo Marg). Just before reaching the Qutb Minar, turn left (east) on to the Badarpur Road, at the far end of which lies Tughluqabad, the vast fourteenth-century fort, with nearby the tomb of Ghiyas-ud-din (pp. 29–30).

Further Reading

History

The history of Delhi, as recounted by scholars, is inseparable from that of northern India in general, so a comprehensive bibliography would be vast and wide. But the successive phases in the city's history are well captured in a handful of well-written studies: Upinder Singh, *Ancient Delhi*, 1999; Khaliq Ahmad Nizami, *Royalty in Medieval India*, 1997; Kishori Saran Lal, *Twilight of the Sultanate*, 1980; Francis Robinson, *The Mughal Emperors*, 2007; T.C.A. Raghavan, *Attendant Lords*, 2017; Jadunath Sarkar, *A Short History of Aurangzeb*, 2009; Audrey Truschke, *Aurangzeb: The Man and the Myth*, 2017; William Dalrymple, *The Last Mughal*, 2006; Percival Spear, *Twilight of the Mughals*, 1951; Narayani Gupta, *Delhi between Two Empires*, 1981.

Architecture: Listings and Handbooks

The definitive catalogue of the city's monuments is: Ratish Nanda, Narayani Gupta and O.P. Jain, *Delhi: The Built Heritage—A Listing*, INTACH, 2 vols, 1999. The classic listing is: Zafar Hasan, *Monuments of Delhi*, 4 vols, 1916–20. The best recent handbooks are: Lucy Peck, *Delhi: A Thousand Years of Building*, 2005; and Swapna Liddle, *Delhi: 14 Historic Walks*, 2011. Two older guides still have value: Percival Spear, *Delhi: Its Monuments and History*, 1943, reprinted 1997; and Y.D. Sharma, *Delhi and Its Neighbourhood*, ASI, 1964/1982. The classics, now themselves historical relics, include H.C. Fanshawe, *Delhi Past and Present*, 1902; Gordon Risley Hearn, *The Seven Cities of Delhi*, 1906; and Gordon Sanderson, *Delhi Fort: A Guide to the Buildings and Gardens*, 1914. A recent book with an engaging narrative approach is Swapna Liddle, *Chandni Chowk: The Mughal City of Old Delhi*, 2017. The work by Percy Brown that is referred to is *Indian Architecture (Islamic Period)*, 1942. Simon Digby's article on the Lodi Gardens is published in *The Bulletin of SOAS*, Vol. 38, No. 3, 1975. Subhash Parihar's article on the Afsarwala mosque is in *Marg*, Vol. 49, No. 4, 1998.

Mughal Court and Culture

As with the city's history, most accounts of Delhi's Mughal culture are embedded in studies of broader reach. A few of the best are: Gavin Hambly, *Cities of Mughul India*, 1968; Bamber Gascoigne, *The Great Moghuls*, 1971; M.M. Kaye, *The Golden Calm: An English Lady's Life in Moghul Delhi*, 1980; Ebba Koch, *Mughal Architecture: An Outline*, 1991; Annemarie Schimmel, *The Empire of the Great Mughals*, 2004; William Dalrymple and Yuthika Sharma (eds), *Princes and Painters in Mughal Delhi, 1707–1857*, 2012; Sadia Dehlvi, *The Sufi Courtyard: Dargahs of Delhi*, 2012.

New Delhi

The best accounts of the planning and building of the new capital are: Robert Grant Irving, *Indian Summer: Lutyens, Baker and Imperial Delhi*, 1981; Gavin Stamp, 'New Delhi' in *Lutyens*, Arts

Council of Great Britain, 1981; Andreas Volwahsen, *Imperial Delhi*, 2002; Aman Nath, *Dome over India: Rashtrapati Bhavan*, 2006; Malvika Singh, *New Delhi: Making of a Capital*, 2009; Dhruva N. Chaudhuri, *New Delhi down the Decades*, 2013; Sumanta K. Bhowmick, *Princely Palaces in New Delhi*, 2016 and Swapna Liddle, *Connaught Place*, 2018.

Modern Architecture

Rahul Khanna, *The Modern Architecture of New Delhi*, 2008, is a general handbook. The careers of two distinguished architects of the city are covered in monographs: Brian Brace Taylor, *Raj Rewal*, 1992; and Stephen White, *Building in the Garden: The Architecture of Joseph Allen Stein in India and California*, 1998. The story of the US Embassy is told in Tom Wolfe, *From Bauhaus to Our House*, 1982.

Urbanism, etc.

Catherine B. Asher, *Delhi's Qutb Complex: The Minar, Mosque and Mehrauli*, 2017; Norma Evenson, *The Indian Metropolis*, 1989; Lawrence J. Vale, *Architecture, Power and National Identity*, 1992; Pradip Krishen, *Trees of Delhi: A Field Guide*, 2006; J.P. Losty, *Delhi 360°: Mazhar Ali Khan's View from the Lahore Gate*, 2012; J.P. Losty (ed.), *Delhi: Red Fort to Raisina*, 2012; Jyoti Hosagrahar, *Indigenous Modernities: Negotiating Architecture and Urbanism*, 2005; Pilar Maria Guerrieri, *Maps of Delhi*, 2017; Pilar Maria Guerrieri, *Negotiating Cultures: Delhi's Architecture and Planning from 1912 to 1962*, 2018.

Selected Novels and Travelogues

Flora Annie Steel, *On the Face of the Waters*, 1896; Ahmed Ali, *Twilight in Delhi*, 1940; Anita Desai, *In Custody*, 1984;

Khushwant Singh, *Delhi: A Novel*, 1990; Ruskin Bond, *Delhi Is Not Far*, 1994/2003; William Dalrymple, *City of Djinns: A Year in Delhi*, 1993; Ranjana Sengupta, *Delhi Metropolitan*, 2007; Sam Miller, *Delhi: Adventures in a Megacity*, 2008; Shamsur Rahman Faruqi, *The Mirror of Beauty*, 2013.

Anthologies of Essays

Khushwant Singh (ed.), *City Improbable*, 2001; Mala Dayal (ed.), *Celebrating Delhi*, 2010; Bharati Chaturvedi (ed.), *Finding Delhi*, 2010; Shveta Sarda (ed. and transl.), *Trickster City*, 2010; Sunil Kumar, *The Present in Delhi's Pasts*, 2011.

Photographic Portraits

Khushwant Singh and Raghu Rai, *Delhi: A Portrait*, 1983; Narayani Gupta and Dilip Bobb, *Delhi Then & Now* (n.d.); Jim Masselos and Narayani Gupta, *Beato's Delhi, 1857 and Beyond*, 1997; Karoki Lewis and Charles Lewis, *Mehrauli: A View from the Qutb*, 2002.

Acknowledgements

I first came to Delhi forty years ago, in 1979, and I have lived on its periphery (in Gurgaon) for the last fifteen. In the course of that time, I have visited the monuments and sites described here countless times. I have profited from the knowledge and insights of the many people with whom I have shared that pleasure. I cannot name them all, but I should like to thank especially the organizers and participants in a series of seminars on Delhi held in recent years at INTACH, including A.G.K. Menon, Swapna Liddle and Annabel Lopez. I thank Kishore Singh at DAG, Rahaab Allana at the Alkazi Collection of Photography, Devika Daulet-Singh of Photoink, and the Trustees of the Maharaja Sawai Man Singh II Museum, for the use of images; Mrinalini Venkateswaran for her feedback on several sections; and Ranjana Sengupta, Anushree Kaushal, Saloni Mital and Ahlawat Gunjan at Penguin Random House.

Index

Abbasid caliphate, 19
Adham Khan, tomb of, 65–66, 148
Advani, L.K., 7, 9
Afghan War, Third, 1919, 108
Afsarwala, 63, 144
Aga Khan Trust for Culture (AKTC), 144–45
Agra, 51, 54, 61, 64, 65, 67, 68, 80
Ahimsa Sthal, Mehrauli, 149
Ahmad Shah (r. 1748–54), 84
Ahmad Shah Abdali, 84–86
Ahmed Ali, *Twilight in Delhi* (1940), 92
Ajmer, 5, 23, 45, 67
Akbar Hotel, Chanakyapuri, 122
Akbar II (r.1806–37), 88
Akbar, 46, 48, 51, 58, 59, 64–68, 81

Alai Darwaza, 17, 27, 147
Alamgir II, 85–86
Alexander the Great, 104
Alexander, 46
All India War Memorial. *See* India Gate
Allahabad, 65, 88
Amazons, 20
Amba Deep tower, 128
Ambala, 94
Anang Pal, 6
Anangpur, 6
Arab Sarai, 63, 144
Archaeological Survey of India, 147–48
Ashoka, Mauryan emperor, 33
Asian Games Village, Siri Fort, 26, 129–30
Ataga Khan's tomb, 65–66, 67, 145
Athpul, 48

Auckland, Lord, 14
Aurangabad, 80
Aurangzeb (r. 1658–1707), 72, 77, 78, 80–81, 82–5, 157
Azad, Maulana, 80
Azim Khan's tomb, Mehrauli, 149

Babri Masjid demolition, 9
Babur, 9, 18, 40, 43, 49–50, 51–54, 56
Badshahpur, 137
Bagh-i-Alam, 162
Bahadar Shah II (r. 1837–57), 88
Bahadur Shah Zafar (r. 1837–57), xi, 56, 59–60, 66, 91
Bahai House of Worship (Lotus Temple), 128–29, 159–61
Baij, Ramkinker, 152
Bairam Khan, 65, 67
Bajpai, Durga, 122
Baker, Herbert, 104–08, 112, 115, 116, 130, 150–51
Balban (r. 1266–87), 21–23
Bangla Sahib Gurdwara, 154, 156
Bangladesh, 120
Bara Gumbad, 41–42, 44
Barani, 28, 35, 36
Baroda House, 151
Batley, Claude, 122
Battle of Khanua (1527), 52
Battle of Panipat 1526, 49–50, 52, 86
1761, 86
Bayana, 54
Belgian Embassy, 124, 158
Bengal, partition, 1905, 99
Bernier, François, 70–71, 73, 77, 80, 137
Besant, Annie, 106
Bharatpur, 14
Bhul-bhulaiyon, 65–66
Bhuta, Vanu G., 159
Bikaner House, 151
Birla House, Tees January Marg, 157, 159
Blomfield, C. Geoffrey, 114, 151, 153
Blomfield, Francis, 114, 151
Bond, Ruskin, *A Flight of Pigeons*, 96
Bose, Subhash Chandra, 143
British annexation of Indian states, 93
British Council, Kasturba Gandhi Marg, 127, 157
British High Commission, 158
British Library, 153
Brown, Percy, 38, 47, 162
Bu Halima's garden, 144

Buddhist stupa, Sanchi, 105
Burhanpur, 68
Byron, Robert, 108, 150

Cathedral Church of the Redemption, 112, 156
Catholic Cathedral of the Sacred Heart, 156
Central Asians, 52
Central Cottage Industries Emporium, 153
Central New Delhi–South, 157–59
Chamber of Princes, 116
Chanakyapuri, 158
Chandigarh, 122
Chandni Chowk, 68–71, 102, 143, 145
Chandragupta II (r. 375–413), 15
Charles, Prince, 134
Chatta Chowk, 72, 74
chaugan, 19
Chauhans, 7
Chaunsath Khamba, 66, 90, 145
Chengiz (popularly Genghis) Khan, 51
Chhatarpur temple, 149
Chiragh Delhi, 43, 44, 45
Chishti order, 23, 45
Chittor, 64

Chor Bazaar, 70, 71
civil disobedience campaign, 116
Colonnello, Tomasso, 151
Company Painting, 91
Congress/Indian National Congress, 78, 100, 120
Connaught Circus, 115
Connaught Place, 142, 156–57
Contractor, Hafeez, 134
Correa, Charles, 126–27, 157
Council House. *See* Parliament House
Crafts Museum, Pragati Maidan, 126
Curzon, Lord, 73, 99–100, 104
Cyber City, 136

Daniell, Thomas and William, 13, 56, 89–90, 148, 153
Dara Shikoh, 81
Dariba Kalan Road, 143
Das, S.K., 146
Daulatabad, 31–32, 80
Delhi
 the British capital, 98–116
 capital of free India, 117–37
 refuges form Lahore and Multan, 117–19

under Punjab jurisdiction, 98
Delhi Development Authority (DDA), 7
Delhi Durbars, 73, 110
   (1903), 99, 101
   (1911), 99, 101, 153
Delhi Gate, 72
Delhi Sultanate, 6, 8, 18
Deolalikar, G.B., 122
Dhillon, Gurbaksh Singh, 78
Dhilu, Raja, 4
Dholpur, 54
Digby, Simon, 42–43
Dilkusha, 66
Disraeli, Benjamin, 98
DLF 'Gateway Tower', 134
Doshi, B.V., 127

East India Company, 88
Eastern and Western Courts, 115
Eden, Emily, 14
Edward VII, 99
Emergency, 1975–77, 120–21

Faiz Bazaar, 69
Farrel, J.G., *The Siege of Krishnapur*, 96
Farrukhsiyar (r.1713–19), 83
Fath Khan, 36

Fazlu'llah, Shaikh (Jamali), 55
Fergana (at the eastern end of present-day Uzbekistan), 52
Fergusson, James, 72, 95
Festivals of India, 130
First War of Independence, 1857 (Sepoy Mutiny), xi, 69, 73, 77, 92–97, 98, 110, 154, 155
Firuz Shah Kotla, 33, 56, 85, 90, 160
Firuzabad, 33
Ford Foundation, 125
Forster, E.M., *A Passage to India*, 96
Fraser, William, 155
French Embassy, 158

Gandhi, Indira, 119
Gandhi, M.K., 96, 109, 116, 157, 159–60
Gandhi, Rajiv, 121
Gandhi, Sanjay, 120–21
George V, King, 99, 101, 109
George, Lloyd, 115
George, Walter, 114–15, 123, 156
Ghalib, Asadullah Khan (1797–1869), 91–92
Ghazi al-Din, 85, 86

Ghulam Qadir, 86–87
Ghurid, 5–6, 8
Godse, Nathuram, 157
Gol Dak Khana, 156
Golconde, Pondicherry, 122
Golden Temple, Amritsar, 121
Golf Links, 146
Grover, Satish, 157
Gujarat, 39, 64
Gujral, Satish, 124, 158
Gurgaon, 134–37, 149
Gwalior, 54, 82
Gymkhana club, 153

Habitat Centre, 145, 146
Hajji Begam, 59
Hall of Nations, Pragati Maidan, 136
Hamid Khan, 40
Hanuman temple, Baba Kharak Singh Marg, 154, 156
Hardinge, Lord, 102–03, 110
Hauz Khas, 26, 35–37; to Tughluqabad, 161–63
Hauz-i-Shamsi, 23, 148
Havell, E.B., 104
Hayat Bakhsh Bagh, 77, 91
Hearn, Gordon Risley, 96
Heber, Reginald, 88
Heinz, Karl, 158

Himachal Bhavan, Mandi House, 157
Hindu and Jain temples, 8
Hindu festivals, 18
Hindu Kush, 4
Hindu-Muslim relations, 9
Hindus, 53
Hindustan Motors, 133
Hodgkin, Howard, 127
Hodson, Captain, 56, 60, 95
Humayun (r.1530–40 and 1555–56), 54–59
Humayun's tomb, xi, 48, 51, 56, 59–64, 67, 85–86, 90, 95, 105, 130, 143–46, 161
Hyderabad, 82
Hyderabad House, 112, 151

Ibn Battuta, 19–20, 23, 30
Iltutmish (r. 1210–36), 13, 16, 17, 19–20, 21, 23, 26, 146
Imperial Assemblage, 98
Independence and Partition, xi
India Gate (All-India War Memorial), x, 105, 108–09, 112, 151, 154
India International Centre (IIC), 125, 145, 146

India Islamic Cultural Centre, 146
Indian Institute of Immunology, 130
Indian Institute of Management, Ahmedabad, 123
Indian National Army, 78
Indian National Congress. *See* Congress
Indira Gandhi Memorial, Safdarjang Road, 158
Indira Gandhi National Centre for the Arts (IGNCA), Janpath, 150–54
Indo-China border dispute and war, 1962, 120
Indo-Islamic architecture, 48
Indo-Pakistan war, 1965, 120
Indo-Saracenic movement, 122
Indraprastha, 58
Inter State Bus Terminus, 122
Intercontinental (now Oberoi) hotel, 122
International Modern Movement, 111, 122, 124, 127
International Network for Traditional Building, Architecture and Urbanism (INTBAU), 134

Irwin, Lord, 116
Isa Khan's tomb, 63, 144
Isami, 21
Islam Shah, 55
Islamic architecture, 12–13
Islamic buildings of India, 12–13
Ismail the Samanid, tomb of, 16–17

Jacob, Samuel Swinton, 155
Jahanara, 64, 143, 145
Jahandar Shah, 83, 87
Jahangir (r. 1605–27), 51, 66–67
Jahangir, Mirza, 88
Jahanpanah, 31, 33, 34
Jai Singh I, 84
Jai Singh II, Maharaja of Jaipur, 84, 153–54
Jaipur, 82
Jaipur House, 114, 151
Jaisinghpura, 84
jal mahal, 91
Jamali-Kamali, tomb of, 54–55, 148
Jami Masjid, 33, 69, 78–79, 95, 141–43
Janpath, 150–54
Jantar Mantar, x, 84, 90, 154
Jats, 85
Jaunpur, 39

Jawaharlal Nehru University, 124
jiziya, 33
Jones, Inigo, 158
Jor Bagh, 43
Journal of the Indian Institute of Architects, 114
Judaeo-Christian tradition, 28

Kabir (1440–1518), 45–46
Kabuli Gate. *See* Khuni Darwaza
Kahn, Louis, 123, 124, 128
Kaiqubad, 22, 24
Kalan Masjid, Nizamuddin, 34
Kalkaji Mandir, 161
Kamali, 55
Kanvinde, Achyut, 128
Kashmir, 67
Kashmiri Gate, 95, 97; and beyond, 154–56
Khairpur, 41, 43
Khalji, Alauddin (r. 1296–1316), 13, 24–27, 31, 35, 44
Khalji, Qutbuddin Mubarak (r. 1316–20), 27
Khaljis and Tughluqs, 24–37, 64
Khan, Aga, 61
Khan, Ghulam Ali, 91

Khan, Hasan-Uddin, 126–27
Khan Jahan Junan Shah, 34
Khan, Mazhar Ali, 91
Khan, Shah Nawaz, 78
Khan, Syed Ahmed, 11, 76, 79
Khirkhi Masjid, 34
Khizr Khan, 38
Khosla, Romi, 128
Khuni Darwaza (Kabuli Gate), 56
Khusrau Khan, 27
Khusrau, Amir, 24–25, 64, 145
Kingsway Camp, 118
Kipling, Rudyard, 58
Kokaltash, Mirza Aziz, 67
Krier, Leon, 134–35, 136
Kuil, 54
Kukreja, C.P., 124, 128
Kuldip Singh, 122

Lahauri, Ustad Ahmad, 142
Lahore, 65
Lahore Gate, 71–72, 74
Lajpat Nagar, 118
Lake, Lord, 87
Le Corbusier, 122, 123, 124, 127
Lerner, Ralph, 153
liberalization of the Indian economy, 130, 133

Life Insurance Corporation building, Connaught Place, 126
Lincoln Memorial, Washington, 109
Lodi, Bahlul (r. 1451–89), 40–43, 44, 47
Lodi Estate, 4, 130, 146
Lodi Gardens, x, 40–41, 43, 46–48, 145
Lodi, Ibrahim (r. 1517–26), 40, 49–50, 52
Lodi Road, 143–46
Lodi, Sikander (r. 1489–1517), 40, 43, 44, 46–48, 51, 148
Lodis, 38–50, 52, 63, 65
Lotus Temple. *See* Bahai House of Worship
Lucknow, 82, 85, 93
Lutyens Bungalow Zone (LBZ), 111, 137
Lutyens, Edwin, 61, 102–12, 114–16, 122, 127, 130, 137, 150–51, 55, 158, 159
Lytton, Lady Emily Bulwer, 106
Lytton, Lord, 98, 106

Madho Singh II, Maharaja of Jaipur, 154
Mah Banu, 67
Mahabharata, 6, 58
Maham Anga, 65
Mahmud of Ghazni, 5
Mahmud, grandson of Firuz Shah Tughluq, 37
Malwa, 39, 64, 67
Mandi House, 157
Mandu, 67
Manik Bagh, 122
Marathas, 85–86, 87
Mary, Queen, 99, 101
Mathura, 84, 143
Medd, Henry, 112, 113
Meena Bazaar, 80
Meerut, 93
Mehrauli, 23, 65, 66, 91, 146–49
Mehrauli Archaeological Park, 148
Metcalfe, Charles, 89
Metcalfe, Thomas, 66, 155
Metro rail system, 133, 141, 157
Mewar, 39
Mirak Mirza Ghiyas, 60
Modern School, 114, 123
Mody, Piloo, 122
Monserrate, Antonio, 56
Montagu–Chelmsford Reforms, 1919, 115
Mother Teresa Crescent, 156
Moti Masjid, 77

Mountbatten, Lord, 116
Mubarak Shah, 39, 40
Mughal Gardens, 110, 114
Mughals, Mughal Dynasty, ix–xii, 4, 6, 8, 9, 12,. 14, 17, 18, 43, 48, 49, 51–81, 98, 101, 105, 127, 130, 142, 144–46, 149, 160; Late Mughals, 82–97
Muhammad bin Sam, the sultan of Ghur, 5–6, 7, 18–19
Muhammad Shah Rangila (r. 1719–48), 83–84, 156
Muhammad, son Balban, 22
Muin-ud-din, Khwaja, 23
Mukherjee, Snehanshu, 151
Mumtaz Mahal (Arjumand Banu Begum), 64, 68
Murshidabad, 82
Museum of Modern Art, New York, 158
Muslim invaders destroyed temples, 9–11
Mutahhar, poet of Kara, 35–36
Muthesius, Eckart, 122
Mutiny Memorial, Kashmiri Gate, 156

Nadir Shah, 83–84, 85
Nagpalji, Baba Sant, 149
Najaf Khan, Mirza, 86
Naqqar Khana, 72–73, 74
Nasiruddin Mahmud (d. 1356, Chiragh-i-Dihli), 45
National Archives, Janpath, 152
National Gallery of Modern Art, 151–52
National Institute of Fashion Technology (NIFT), 127
National Museum, Janpath, 152
National Science Centre, Pragati Maidan, 128
National Zoological Park (Delhi Zoo), 160–61
Nehru Place, 123
Nehru, Jawaharlal, 41, 115, 116, 117, 119, 158
Netaji Subhash Road, 143
New Delhi Municipal Council (the old Civic Centre), 122
Nicholson, John, 95, 155
Nizami, 46
Nizamuddin Auliya (d. 1325), 25, 31, 44–45, 63–64, 66, 145
Nizamuddin village, 34, 64, 145, 161
North-West Frontier, 108

North-West Provinces, 98
Nowruz celebrations, 18

Old Delhi, 69, 129, 137

Pakistan, 117–18
Pakistani High Commission, 158
Parks, Fanny, 14, 76, 88
Parliament House (Sansad Bhavan), 105, 108, 115–16, 151
partition and growth, independent India, 117–38
Patiala House, 151
Persian customs and ceremonies, 18
Pevsner, Sir Nikolaus, 111
Prasad, Shiv Nath, 122, 146, 157
Princes Place, 151
Prinsep, James, 34
Prithviraj Chauhan, 5, 7–9, 11
Punjab, 94, 98
Punjabi Bagh, 118
Punjabi identity, 119
Purana Qila (Old Fort), xi, 6, 13, 56–57, 90, 110, 118, 160

Qila Rai Pithora (Lal Kot), 7–9, 33

Qila-i-Kuhna Masjid, 57
Qudsia Bagh, 90, 155–56
Quli Khan's tomb, 66, 148
Qutb Minar, 8–9, 11–16, 23, 26, 29, 33, 39, 45, 49, 57, 66, 90, 105, 146–49, 163. *See also* Mehrauli
Qutb Sahib's dargah, 148
Qutb-ud-din Aibak, 6, 8–9, 11, 13, 18–21, 103
Qutb-ud-din Bakhtiyar Kaki, Khwaja (d. 1236), 23, 45
Quwwatu'l-Islam mosque, 8, 13, 15, 20, 26, 34, 137, 146

Rabindra Bhavan, Mandi House, 125, 157
Rahim Khan, Abdur (Khan-i-Khanan), 67
Rahman, Habib, 80, 125, 157
Raisina hill, 110, 150
Rajghat to Lotus Temple, 159–61
Rajinder Kumar, 123
Rajinder Nagar, 118
Rajon-ki-Bain, Mehrauli, 148
Rajpath (formerly called Kingsway), 108, 150–54. *See also* Janpath

Rajput architecture, 11, 91
Rajputs, 20, 23, 52
Ramananda, 45
Ramanathan, A.R., 151
Rang de Basanti (2006), 109
Rang Mahal, 88
Rashtrapati Bhavan (Viceroy's House), xii, 102, 105, 106, 109, 114, 116, 150, 158
Ratan Singh, 123
Raymond, Antonin, 122
Raziya (r. 1236–40), 20–21
Red Fort, x, 68–78, 80, 83, 86, 88, 91, 93, 95, 101, 141–43
Regent, Prince, 151
religious differences in India, 9, 11
Rewal, Raj, 129–30, 136, 146, 153, 158
Roe, Thomas, 67
Roman Forum, 103
Round Table Conferences, 116
Roy, Jamini, 152
Rukn-ud-din Firuz, 20
Russell, Robert Tor, 115, 156

Sachdev, Jasbir and Rosemary, 123
Safavids of Persia, 83
Safdarjang's tomb, 85, 146
Sahba, Fariborz, 128–29, 161
Sahgal, Prem, 78
Salimgarh, 68
Samarkand, 37, 51, 52, 53, 60
Sanderson, Gordon, 147–48
Sanga, Rana of Mewar, 49–50, 52
Sanjar, Seljuq Sultan, tomb of, 17
Sansad Bhavan. *See* Parliament House
Sayyid, Muhammad Shah (d. 1445), 40, 46
Sayyids, 38–50, 63, 65, 88
Scindias, 82
SCOPE office complex, 130, 131
Secretariats, xii, 105, 108, 109, 150
Seljuq Persia, 11
Sepoy Mutiny, 1857. *See* First War of Independence
Shah Alam (d. 1451), 39
Shah Alam (r. 1759–1806), 86–89
Shah Jahan (r. 1627–58), x, 51, 64, 68–69, 72, 76, 78, 80–81, 84, 143
Shah Nama, 18
Shah, Fath Ali, 150–51

Shahjahanabad, 56, 66, 68, 89–90, 118, 130, 141–43
Shahpur Jat, 26
Sharp, Henry, 43
Sheesh Gumbad, 42, 43, 44
Sher Shah. *See* Sur, Sher Shah
Shergil, Amrita, 152
Shoosmith, A.G., 112, 115
Shri Ram Arts Centre, Mandi House, 122, 157
Sikander Begum of Bhopal, 21
Sikandra, 46, 67
Sikri, 54
Simla, 94, 100
Simpson, William, 153
Siri, 25–26, 31, 33
Skinner, James, 14, 155
Slave dynasty, 5–29
Smith, Robert, 13, 15, 17, 57, 147, 155
Solomon, King, 20
Spastics Society school, 128
St James's Church, Kashmiri Gate, 14, 155
St Martin's Garrison Church, 112, 115
St. Stephen College, 156
Stamp, Gavin, 112
Steel, Flora Annie, *On the Face of the Waters*, 96
Stein, Joseph Allen, 41, 48, 125, 145–46, 157

Stone, Edward Durrell, 158–59
Sufism, 44, 45
Sultan Ghari, 20
Summerson, Sir John, 111
Sunder Nagar nursery, 144
Sunni Muslims, 82
Sur Dynasty, Surs, 43, 55, 59, 65, 160
Sur, Sher Shah (Sher Khan), 55–58, 63
Suraj Kund, 7
Suraj Pal, 7
Sydney Opera House, 129

Tagore, Abanindranath, 152
Taj Mahal, 17, 42, 48, 68, 77, 129, 142, 144
Teen Murti Bhavan, 115, 158
Thapar, Romila, 126
Tibet House, Lodi Road, 122, 146
Timur (Tamburlaine), 37, 38, 40, 51–52, 60, 64, 82
Tolstoy Marg, 153
Tomar Rajputs, 7, 8, 15, 49
Tomar, Man Singh, 49
Trafalgar Square, London, 109
Treaty of Allahabad, 1765, 86
Triveni Kala Sangam, Mandi House, 125, 157

Tughluq Shah, 28
Tughluq, Firuz Shah (r. 1351–88), 13, 32–36, 37, 45, 160, 161
Tughluq, Ghiyasud-din (r. 1320–25), 28–31, 44, 46, 163
Tughluq, Muhammad bin (r. 1325–51), 28–29, 31–32, 44, 80, 133
Tughluqabad, 29, 31, 33, 161–63
Tughluqs, 24–37, 64, 86

Ujjain, 84
Urdu poetry, 91

Varanasi, 84
Vasant Kunj, 20
Venturi, Robert, 111
Viceroy's House. See Rashtrapati Bhavan
Victoria Memorial Hall, Calcutta, 104

Victoria, Queen, 98
Vikramaditya, 49
Vishnupada hill, 15
Vistara (1986), 126

Willingdon, Lady, 150
Wolfe, Tom, 158
World Bank office, Lodi Estate, 130, 146
World War I, 108, 115, 147
World War II, 78, 116
Wren, Christopher, 106, 108, 158

Yamuna, x, 5, 22, 33, 48, 56, 68, 70, 87, 144, 159

Zamin, Imam, tomb of, 17
Zauq, Mohammed Ibrahim (1788–1855), 91
Zinat Mahal, 93

PR
7794
1/15/19